Gloryland
Reprise

Preface

To the few who love me and whom I love –
to those who feel rather than those
who think – to the dreamers and those
who put faith in dreams as in the only realities –
I offer this Book of Truths,
not in its character of Truth-Teller;
but for the Beauty that abounds
in its Truth; constituting it true.
To these I present the composition
as an Art-Product alone: –
let us say as a Romance;
or, if I be not urging too lofty a claim,
as a Poem.

What I here propound is true: –
therefore it cannot die: –
or if by any means it be now trodden down
so that it die, it will
"rise again to the Life Everlasting."

Nevertheless, it is as a Poem only
that I wish this work to be judged after I am dead.

– E.A.P. (Edgar Allan Poe)

Gloryland Reprise

Drew Signor

*Walking the Southern Arizona Wilderness
and the Spiritual Implications of Landscape*

Gloryland Reprise
© 2021 Drew Signor

Other books by Drew Signor:
"Sweat of the Sun, Tears of the Moon" –
30 Years of Songs, Essays and Insights,
the Artist and his Craft

Gloryland Reprise
ISBN: 978-1-09837-899-8

Book design and illustration
© 2021 kate horton
kmhGraphics

OCOTILLO
Drew Signor
Benson, Arizona

Dedication

To my father
John J. Signor,
who was forever in love
with the sound of words and their meaning.

"I am what has become of me . . .
a man who lives in the desert."

– Richard Shelton

In the Mornings of Home

*"I have often said that the sole cause
of man's unhappiness is that he
does not know how to stay quietly in his room."*

– Blaise Pascal

Santa Catalinas

It snowed on the Santa Catalinas today.
Bright sun on the clouds as they faded away.
Left the snowline high above the desert floor.

"The Lord by wisdom founded the earth;
by understanding
He established the heavens;
by His knowledge
the deeps broke forth,
and the clouds drop down the dew."

– Proverbs 3:19-20

Long ago in the dream time,
God made the world when
no one was looking.

Double Granite

"And what have we to do with talk of genus and species!
He to whom the Eternal Word speaketh
is free from multiplied questionings.
From this One Word are all things, and all things, speak of Him;
and this is the Beginning which also speaketh unto us.
No man without Him understandeth or rightly judgeth.
The man to whom all things are one, who bringeth
all things to one, who seeth all things in one,
he is able to remain steadfast of spirit, and rest in God...
Let all doctors hold their peace;
let all creation keep silence before Thee:
speak Thou alone to me."

– Thomas à Kempis / *The Imitation of Christ*

The Dragoons

*"Once in his life a man ought to concentrate his mind upon the
remembered earth… He ought to give himself up to a
particular landscape in his experience, to look at it from
as many angles as he can, to wonder about it, to dwell upon it.
He ought to imagine that he touches it with his hands
at every season and listens to the sounds
that are made upon it. He ought to imagine the
creatures there and all the faintest motions of the wind.
He ought to recollect the glare of the moon
and all the colors of the dawn and dusk."*

– N. Scott Momaday / *The Way to Rainy Mountain*

The Guadalupes

*"The aesthetic sense – the power to enjoy through
the eye, the ear and imagination –
is just as important a factor
in the scheme of human happiness as the
corporeal sense of eating and drinking;
but there has never been a time
when the world would admit it."*

– John C. Van Dyke

Down Deep in the Dell

CONTENTS

"Have you not known?
Have you not heard?
The Lord is the everlasting God,
the Creator of the ends of the earth."
– Isaiah 40:28-29

Flooding on the San Pedro

"*Correspondences, are representations of things
Spiritual and Celestial in things Natural.*"
– Emanuel Swedenborg

It's an eddy in time,
Where blue-mountains climb
And quiet canyons wait.

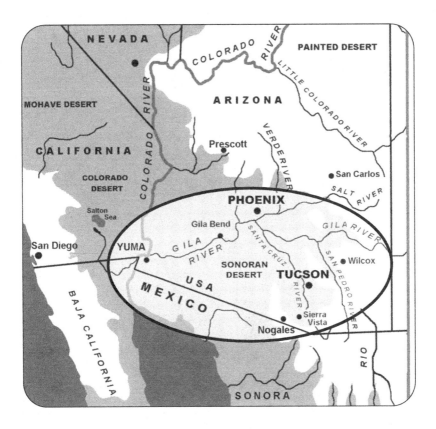

Theater of Operations

This is a General Map to show my travels in this book.

Gloryland Reprise

Chapter 1:
This Gloryland

In the shadows of the first mornings light
Sunbeams cut the canyons from a deep dyed blue
Ragged mountains poke their heads through porcelain clouds
And the sun's fire sparks their glow and newborn day
Wild rivers sing songs and birds sing along in harmony
The rewards of walking this wilderness – This Gloryland

It's work but worth it as you wander this wild ground
The soothing silence stirs the soul for the challenge of the call
Dreamscapes of color on a canvas of constant change
Timeless theatrics in this theater that the Lord set in play
How long do mountains stand, how long
This beauty and the unexplained that leads me on
The rewards of walking this wilderness – This Gloryland

I know that urban minds don't understand
Sierras packed with snow this grand
That feed these streams where lion seek their quarry
Or the starry nights that burn and blaze
Beyond this creeping city maze
That kills This Gloryland to leave us sorry
And I am the voice of one singing in this wilderness
What God has made let no man put asunder

In the evenings, when the gleaming sun shafts play
On the saddles and peaks seared with the last dazzling beam
Retreating ranges cool their colors in a purple parade
Clouds brightly bleeding pull the curtain
On the sun's passion play
Then constellations sing and shine
And a campfire will keep you fine until the dawn
The rewards of walking this wilderness – This Gloryland,
This Gloryland.

Aravaipa Canyon

Chapter 2:
Westward Bound

Westward bound... there's a peace I've found
On a road that's westward bound
On a road that's westward bound

I've always been one to roam and wander
And I guess it's always gonna be that way
Born for some rim-rock and a river with a bend
Empty deserts fenced with snowy-mountain crowns

I want a road that's westward bound
I need a prairie rolling gold or green
I need big mountains that can frame my horizons
With cutting-canyons where the cataracts sound
I want a road that's westward bound

Westward bound... there's a peace I've found
On a road that's westward bound
So if I'm not around... I'm sure to wander
I'm bound for any road just west of town

Westward bound... there's a peace I've found
On a road that's westward bound
On a road that's westward bound
On a road that's westward bound.

In my imagination all my roads are headed west.

There's a change in Arizona sand
I'm gonna go as planned
I'm takin' my leave... I won't be back again
There's really no tellin' when you might see me again
No tellin' when.

Chapter 3:
Summer Rain

*"The landscape that is simplest in form and the finest
in color is by all odds the most beautiful."*

— John C. Van Dyke

In the evenings after dinner, as the day draws to a close, I step out my door cross Sonoita Creek and climb a niggling knoll to watch a setting sun.

From this vantage point I can look out across our peaceful pastoral valley and the town of Patagonia. Blue-mountains fence the horizon. The rippling roll of grassy, open oak-wooded-hillock, preordains a creek and its cotton-wooded course through a perfect hollow.

The vault of welkin-blue and its cloud-colored splendor with the prim pure rays of culminating sunlight, paint a necromantic mixture of pigment across the firmament of such transcendent glory that only seeing would be, believing. Each evening I see and yet cannot believe, that such a landscape of poetry, such lambent-light-seraphic breathed, or possibly, but not certainly, was permitted to persist outside the purview of Heaven itself.

No clever manipulation of vocabulary, no manner of linguistic craftiness, could begin to define the keen colors that hang each evening in the perfected atmosphere or describe what this beauty does to my spirit. To put it simply, rather than struggle for words I cannot find, it makes me want to go walking, to walk endlessly onward.

For most of the year, this bucolic landscape of prairie-earth and wood is painted in golden hues, but with the coming of summer rains, grass carpets are transformed from a thing already haughty and handsome, into stunning succulent neon green pastures filled with flowers and steeped in the fragrances of summer.

I guess one is always surprised with the change of seasons. Not that they will change, but that they are always more lovely than we remember them. But the malachite-meads and meadows that stretch out before me, that roll like a Kansas sea of wheat, rank and dark, falls on the retina with a genuine surprise. I stare at this landscape and the canopy of colored clouds strewn across the Eden-sky, believing that such light tinge tone and tincture cannot abide beyond the boundaries of some drug-induced state. The truth is stranger than fiction.

It is nothing more than summer. More beautiful than summers past. It is nothing more than summer, beautiful summer.

> *For me, it's just the walking… walking*
> *And this thought… I just might not return.*

Chapter 4:
A Heart in Two Places

It's been so long, I don't recall
Just when I felt the road first called my name

But there's just somethin' in this restless soul
And those I love no doubt complain
But I feel the need to be a wanderin' somewhere
So I hope this song explains
Cause I got a heart... I got a heart in two places

Sometimes I wonder how it came to be
Me lovin' trains... the road... and topography
This endless yearnin' in my heart to free
These songs that flow from deep inside of me
Still, every callin' has its heartache
Every wanderer is lonesome... every cowboy's missin' home
And I got a heart... I got a heart in two places

I guess you let a restless heart roam a while
The open road a sojourner's domicile... no way to reconcile
The folks you love and the dreams that call
And I got a heart... I got a heart in two places
Broken in two places

It's been so long, I don't recall
Just when I felt the road first called my name
But there's just somethin' in this restless soul
And those I love no doubt complain
But I feel the need to be a wanderin' somewhere
So I hope this song explains
Cause I got a heart... I got a heart in two places
Broken in two places... In two places.

Chapter 5:
Beautiful Things

"There is a special kind of beauty
for every hour the mountain knows,
beauty which man perceives without participating,
beauty to which he feels a stranger."

– Mary Austin / *The Land of Journey's Ending*

Arizona is at least as much a place in my head and heart as it is a place in reality. The reality is so rewarding and it is the foundation on which I have set a large portion of my life.

All I ever wanted to do was to write songs and take a walk somewhere. The world is not interested in such craziness. Walking Arizona has provided me an unending adventure and a wellspring of song writing inspiration. It is a station steeped in an eternal beauty, an undying mystery. It is theater for the imagination. I have let my feet and my mind wander.

I am the least practical person I ever met, as evidenced from the fact that I am on my fourth decade of writing songs, with the full knowledge that no amount of talent, determination or dogged pursuit of my goal can bring this dream to fruition as a working reality. I remain undaunted for one reason only. It is a natural calling; I wouldn't know who I was if couldn't pick up a guitar. I have pursued my craft with an honest and pure heart for the shear love and joy of doing it.

I have pursued walking with the same enthusiasm, for the same reasons. It is a natural calling; I wouldn't know who I was if I couldn't take a walk. For me, there has always been an inherent emotional and spiritual response to landscape which pulls me into it like gravity. Any interesting landscape would do. Preferably a western landscape. But if I lived in Scotland or Spain in Appalachia or Argentina, or call the tune, my life would be the same. I would be walking and fashioning songs. The walking and the writing go hand in hand like a marriage.

The adventure of walking lends itself to romanticism. The glory of creation lends itself to spiritual inspiration. The act of walking fetches a clear mind. My natural joyous response to all this beauty is spontaneous melody.

Fortunately, the artist has license to create out of things around him, that which he will. Living in Arizona has given me a lot to work with, a large and diverse canvas from which to draw. But the wonderful wistful-world I have created in my own imagination is at least as real, as the real wonderful world and sometimes it's hard for me to distinguish between the two.

Sadly, there are things I dislike about the Grand Canyon State as well, mostly man's doing, things I wish I could change, but my impractical artistic outlook allows me to overlook the unpleasant and see only the beautiful. The futility of writing songs, now and then, comes and slaps me upside the head, and this disquieting realization proves to me how much I am living in a province of my own fabrication and how much there is I cannot reconcile.

Arizona remains an extraordinary locality for an extraordinary number of reasons, and for all those reasons, I love it with spunk and pluck, as directing principle and polestar. I was born for the place. I am certain, if you took out of the equation my love for singing and writing songs, this wayward-walking and Arizona itself, my life would cease to exist, at least as I have known it or ever wanted it to be.

This book is a collection of some of my tales, some of my lyrics, some attentions – a sketch along the way.

I boast of no talent but a great love. I am a simple man in every way and in every respect. Writing this strikes me as a bit pretentious. I most humbly consider myself a singer songwriter, wilderness wanderer, a kind of ambling Johnny Appleseed and resident theologian. Being *Swedenborgian* in my outlook explains quite a bit.

I am certainly not a historian, scientist, biologist, botanist, or geologist. I have always been less concerned about the specific statistics and facts about an individual matter, though undeniably important, but as to the inherent truth and spirit of things. Nonetheless, all these subjects very much interest me. And as they relate to the topic at hand, I could recommend a hundred books that would be informative. I can bring nothing

8

to the table in this regard.

This book is not about any place in particular, though every chapter is about a particular place. It is certainly not a book about maps, or what road to take, what trail to walk, what mountains to climb. The local bookstore can provide twenty good reads in this department.

The purpose of writing is an excuse to talk about beautiful things, the art of this creation and a passing note on the spiritual implications of landscape.

Apart from the singularly striking and uncommon components that make this a magical land, I love Arizona first and foremost, for the art of the place, the shear esthetics of this creation. It is the color of the air and the light in the canyons. I am less an artist, than I am one who appreciates good art and sees it in most everything. From the exultant to the mundane, everything in my eye has an esthetic purposeful balance. And like all good art, everything is wrapped in metaphor and the more I look, the more I mark and mind.

If you want to kill a party or a friendship you can bring up theology. Everyone is so fixed in what he or she believes and so convinced the other guy is full of it, that all you end up with is a fight. This wearies me terribly. Relax; I'm not an evangelist. I write to convince no one of anything, but to express what it is that motivates and moves me in regards to landscape. And this passing thought, that has so enhanced my appreciation of nature and has lifted my mind above the merely natural things placed before me, which in and of themselves are marvelous and remarkable beyond words.

There is more to God than I'll ever know. In his infinite love and wisdom his methods complex and manifold and yet surprisingly simple. But in regards to the art of landscape: nothing works as well as this inventive natural canvas and has not God's originative spiritual hand in it. It is the artist's job to express and to comment on this truth and the scientist to establish it. Many will laugh or scoff at my naivete'. But for those who believe, there are more than enough proofs from

9

which to build a foundation of faith and for those who do not, all the proofs in the world are not enough.

It is no coincidence that every civilization and every religion around the world looks up at the mountain and sees its god there. I maintain, though this is by no means original thought; there is an inherent spiritual correspondence with the natural formation, which is a match and immaterial-metaphor a paragon and allegory, reflecting a deeper spiritual reality.

The stumbling block comes when you start believing that the natural object is worthy of worship, or sacred in itself, or that God resides there. No more than an artist, who creates something beautiful, resides in the art he has fashioned; it is clearly reflective of every intent and purport of its maker.

If passed masters use parable and metaphor to discern and disclose, then surely the Supreme Artist, the source from which all things spring – and in whom we live and move and have our being – has fashioned nature in such a way, apart from the obvious purposeful practicalities of creation and if understood in its proper light, as a kind of spiritual metaphor to reveal a higher truth.

"All that is, comes from a marriage of love and wisdom in use. Nothing can exist in the natural world that does not have its connection with the spiritual world; hence is every cause that accomplishes an effect." Nature is the glove a spiritual hand is wearing – nature a foundry for the spirit. If we could lift this material veil, we would then comprehend clearly, that in every created thing hatched and brought into existence, there is something reflecting our Creator, His divine intentions and ourselves categorically. "For all nature is a theater representative of the Lord's Kingdom."

I'm convinced as well that everyone knows this innately without talking about it. It is and it isn't explicit. We sense and perceive it in nature; it is almost palpable, and yet it doesn't quite enter the mind. Sometimes, until a statement is made on a given subject, it doesn't become a tangible idea on which the mind can rest.

Just as music is pure emotion put to melody and the emotional response to it moves us to the crux and core of our being. As great art lifts the spirit and the mind of man in higher import, a pith-noble-essence and weight, beatitudes beyond oneself, so the art of this masterful creation is doing the same. And this spiritual tugging at our hearts and our emotional response to beautiful things, as when we stand by a river, or walk through a forest, or look up at the mountain, is both a conscious and unconscious, reciprocal interplay between the Creator and the created.

"If mountains reflect celestial love and the hills below them, the spiritual; if natural water, corresponds to spiritual truth; if rocks, signify faith; if animals, reflect (man's) varying affections and the trees, perception and knowledge; birds, intellectual things; if gardens, groves and parks, intelligence." Then landscape becomes a stage integrating a metaphysical parallel reflecting a measure of meaning in purpose and plan, an analogue, like an image of God in a mirror, a place where mountains and rivers are spirit condensed.

This grand sweep and wide array of diversified landscapes that Arizona has to offer makes this school of thought all the more dramatically pronounced and poignant. (Arizona macrocosms range from Arctic tundra to sub-tropical deserts, and every conceivable landscape betwixt Canada and Mexico. Each world its own world. Five worlds in one.)

I don't want to pummel my premise; if things are beautiful just because they are beautiful, than so be it. I am intensely and affectionately moved by this splendid art coming into being, and I can't help but within me see cunning spiritual occurrence and circumstance the more I gaze, contentedly, this natural painting. This pleases my spirit no end and makes me think and ponder beautiful things.

Though I was born here in spirit, like everyone else I came from another place, Pennsylvania. But I've been an Arizonan more than forty years and this makes me a native. I feel I know the whereabouts well, at least the part beyond the road.

I spent most of my time residing in Tucson and San Manuel and the unpeopled parts of the San Pedro River Valley, though

11

I spent a remarkable year in Patagonia. I was Thoreau with a guitar. Fighting wildfires for the state, writing some wonderful songs and walking every inch of Santa Cruz County. I have also drifted back and forth at times to the East Coast, both to earn some money and in pursuit of my mythical music career.

I walked long and hard across Arizona for ten years. I never kept a journal, because I was so intent upon writing songs and so believed, as I still do, that I could translate my love into something tangible both for myself and an audience – the grand illusion. So some gratifying walks got away without ever being recorded. After a decade, I wrote a few things down just for prank and practice and a few of these I share with you now. The chapters were written at the while the walks were taken and improved over time. It matters not when I rambled and roamed, nor my precise coordinates, for apart from where the cities are destroying it, This Gloryland remains still touched and timeless.

While reviewing these journals, I got to thinking and remembering all the places I've been and walked. It's amazing how far you can get if you just put one foot in front of another.

For example, in a four-month segment in the 80s, I had walked and climbed in eleven, different mountain ranges. Logged ninety miles traversing three different desert river systems. Nearly froze to death in the conifer forests atop the Guadalupes in west Texas and visited the Pinacate in Mexico. I have sustained this kind of pace over three decades. It has not seemed at all like a marathon, but a steady plodding along for the shear wonder and joy of it.

The bottom line is this: there is a winsome world out there, you fill it with your own personal epic adventure. You make it up as you go along. Go and explore. Leave the car where it is. Take a walk.

"Geography is simply a visual form of theology."

– Jon Levenson

Buehman Creek

Chapter 6:
There I Go Again

Go hang a sliver of moon in the dawn of a western sky
Let the road run long . . . khaki colored prairies wide
Set mountain row on row . . . and there I go again

Somewhere a glacier slides . . . somewhere the skies all blue
Somewhere a spangled river runs beneath the rim-rock's hue
Archaic canyons glow . . . well, there I go again

"There's a poetry about the lonely places
And there are visions in the hills
For those who have eyes to see"
Homilies . . . living truth and wisdom vested
In the psalms of rocks and rills

Somewhere that glory waits . . . though be it far from here
Beyond blue mountain borders beckon new frontiers
Should the wild wind blow . . . well, there I go again
So whither the wind should blow . . . well, there I go again
There I go again.

John C. Van Dyke, was an art critic
who wandered across Arizona's deserts at the dawn
of the last century and penned an artful book, "The Desert."
I was so impressed by his observations and his lyrical prose
that I wanted to sing what he wrote.
As a songwriter, I have gleaned a great cache of jewels
from his treasure and called it my own,
as well as this wonderful quote.

Chapter 7:
Like This Feelin' Free

When there's flowers on the palo verde
And springtime stretches west the Rio Grande
Send my friends, they'll show you where to find me
As I cross this land

When winter's cold has crested snow above me
Far below across the plain I spy
Make this soul into a song that's singin'
With wings that could fly
To that snowy mountain perch
Down to broad valleys below
To bring a song of hope
Of trucks and men and rivers that flow
This feelin' I've got to go

Like a siren's call, I hear faintly... I long to see
Thundershowers brush the desert bloomin'
Like this dry land this thirsty soul it drinks
In all its beauty and God's purpose shinin'
And it makes me think
That I like this feelin free... I'm like the wind and the rain
Some restless tumbleweed
I'm a trucker's-wheels hummin' parade
And I'm rollin' away

When there's flowers on the palo verde
And springtime stretches west the Rio Grande
Send my friends, they'll show you where to find me
As I cross this land.

Kielberg Canyon

Chapter 8:
The American Ghost

"The cry of the mountain lion is difficult to describe,
but one recognizes it quickly enough when he hears it.
It is sometimes the scream but more often the yowl of an enormous
cat. Heard in the night it is perturbing, notwithstanding your
knowledge that the lion never attacks man. You know that,
but does the lion know it?"

– John C. Van Dyke / *The Open Spaces*

Morning sun spilling over the ragged edges of the Galiuro Mountains as the truck trundles up Bingham Ranch road to the gates of Kielberg Canyon – and an unexpected surprise.

I leave the truck on the high-broad shoulders of the canyon's entrance and drop into the boulder-strewn arroyo and begin wading through rocks that stand about my height.

Stepping into a small rock room, phone-booth sized, with a boulder in front and one on either side, meaning to climb through in my procession up the canyon. I open my eyes from a blink, to find a long fur-train of tendon and muscle drifting past my field of vision. Time passes before my brain can figure out what my eyes are seeing.

It's a lion! My heart pounding with the rush and realization, as it lands on a boulder inches from my eyes and is gone. I leap over the rocks, as the lion did, to see big furry paws and powerful legs bounding over rubble, a long tail trailing into brush a short distance ahead. In hot pursuit, even though the country is open, it is not to be found.

Almost twenty years wandering Arizona back country, I never saw a lion. The signs are everywhere – the kills, the scat, the tracks ubiquitous. One never sees a lion. The American Ghost. With this sudden apparition, a very exciting five seconds.

Revelation in its size and silence; the giant cat never made a sound, not scrambling out from under my feet, flying through the air or dashing away. Imagine; deer quietly grazing never know it's coming. There is a moment of being startled as I was, and it's over. Fortunately for me, the lion just wanted to get away. Had he not made his move the moment he did, we would have occupied the same space at the same time. Warning: a rock-cage-tangle with a cougar is not recommended.

Just beyond where I can't find the lion, a dry waterfall has been carved from monolithic blocks of rhyolite and obsidian, chiseling a cistern of stagnant green water and a desperate oasis. In the hundred-degree temperatures, deer come in for a drink. Lions come for dinner.

I climb steep walls, circumnavigating the canyon's box, dropping back in and wandering for miles in a rapturous joy. Not just because of the lion, though my face is flushed and adrenaline flows – it is this captivating and peculiar place. Beauty the gravity pulling me onward through marvelous rock architecture and the desert's strange flora.

Saguaros stand on stark slopes. Handsome oak groves cowering in shaded nooks. Stagnate water pools carved into the canyon's red floor, cottonwood and willow abiding in the rocky chaos, awash in a blast of brilliant sun. Beyond the stream where the water should be, vines scamper and grasses advance. The pleasing intricacies and primitive aesthetics, engaging canyon walls climb, enlarging my spirit to the scale of this creation.

The land is older than I can imagine and the ghosts of men long gone haunt these rocky recesses. A good distance up the canyon a grotto, where Anasazi pictographs of lizards and deer record some history. An ancient corncob on the cave's floor, an extraordinary find.

More miles with the canyon escalating, as gnarled grabbling oaks swell over the rising hills. Though the desert retreats reluctantly, on hot sunny slopes only a few trees stand up to the challenge in a blaze of gold grass. The clarion air and radiant sun, the wilderness quickened in the dazzle.

Eventually the canyon closes against an exalted gulf of stone, which harbors a spare shaded stand of mature maple trees.

Bear scat on the groves leafy floor. Maples on the desert's edge? Astounding. I'm as excited about the discovery of these determined trees, as I am the mountain lion. There are more secrets in these mountains than men could know.

It is very hot and I've come a good distance. My retreat through the canyon unfolds like a dream, a near swoon in the stifling heat and celestial light, where the world shimmers like a mirage on hot macadam.

The life and death struggles are rarely seen. Wilderness days unfold in a calm and peaceful manner and it often seems that nothing happens here at all. Halfway home, a startled coyote dissolves into the brush and brier. I discover a lion-kill beside a stilled water-pool canopied of stately oaks where ravens scavenge the last of the flesh from the last of the bones. A lot does happen here, but it happens in short bursts.

The day is long and the miles as well. I hobble over the last ridge and peer into the rock-box where I saw the lion. A diamondback rattles a warning.

A three-quarter-moon pops over the Galiuros sharp edge like the sun just hours before. The truck trundles down the road for home, leaving mountains to moon glow, coyotes, lions and the ghosts of men to wander.

"Puma, cougar, catamount,
Felis concolor, the shy,
secret shadowy lion of the new world,
four- or five-feet long plus a yard
of black-tipped tail,
weighs about what a woman weighs,
lives where the deer live
from Canada to Chile, but always shier,
always fewer, the color of dry leaves, dry grass."

– Ursula K Le Guin / *"May's Lion,"*
Buffalo Gals and Other Animal Presences

Chapter 9:
Day In, Day Out

Day in… day out… I love what love's about
These mountains… these streams… the songs they sing
The dreams I dream… day in… day out… day in
Day in… day out… I love what love's about
Mother Earth… Father Sky…the seasons turn
The years gone by… day in… day out… day in

Day in… day out… upon this land I sense God's purpose
In all He is fashioned… clearly shown
Day in… day out… I know
Like a field here I've been planted
Unto a harvest we've been sown
Day in… day out… I love what love's about
The rivers turn… the stars that shine… this prairie green
Your unseen hand in mine… day in… day out… day in

Day in… day out… upon this land I sense God's purpose
In all He is fashioned… clearly shown
Day in… day out… I know
Like a field here I've been planted
Unto a harvest we've been sown
Day in… day out… I love what love's about
These mountains… these streams… the songs they sing
The dreams I dream… day in… day out… day in
Day in… day out… day in.

Still, a man must make his own choice work
And mine… to walk and write
I stand and smile… I sing and say
When things go bad he needs someone
For what's a man, but faith
With dreams to follow anyway.

Chapter 10:
Muleshoe Ranch

"If there is magic on this planet, it is contained in water."

– Loren Eiseley / *The Immense Journey*

The Galiuro Mountains may well be one of Southern Arizona's best kept secrets. My hope for the range, that it will remain so. It has earned a special place in my heart not just for its rugged austere beauty, but more out of a respect for its deceptive topography and this pensive, disconcerting uneasiness that it leaves in my craw.

The mountains have everything but real height, what they lack in stature, other attributes make up for this one shortcoming. Miles of saguaro and creosote line the banks of the San Pedro River, its western boundary. Thick forests of oak choke its rigorous canyons. Higher still, Arizona cypress and ponderosa pine cling to the heights. To the east, stretch golden prairies. The spectacular canyon Aravaipa to the north, a mini Grand Canyon and a national treasure; the Winchester Mountains are a separate range, but somehow attached to the Galiuros southern end, together form a wide array of flora and fauna in its diversified terrain of some one-thousand square-miles.

One hundred-and-twelve-degree waters spring from a hillside in the dry wash of Hot Springs Canyon. Muleshoe Ranch consists of a few buildings, this steaming trickle of scalding water and the fifty-thousand acres that surround it. The Nature Conservancy, an organization that purchases endangered lands, manages there, that the seven perennial streams that flow through these frenetic Galiuro canyons and the fish in them might be protected.

I cross the dry wash, up and over a high desert hill and drop into Bass Canyon. From the crest of the knoll, a distant seven-thousand-foot escarpment built with tarnished stripes of tan and maroon rock. The foreground a-jumble of large well-rounded hills, half stone half grass, like a clump of burnt biscuits tardily retrieved from the oven. In the seams between

21

each bun, forests of cottonwood work their way through canyon crevice and present a clear and convincing map of the extensive river systems that run through this spacious stone quilt.

In the canyon, I stash my pack and walk up the rills for a while. Deliberate and dignified, the crowned jewels of the waterway, cottonwood take an imposing stand stream-side. The bare, white bark of Arizona sycamores, stark against a blue sky, their creamed coffee leaves crunch under foot and clash with the creek's conversation.

After investigating a dilapidated ranch house, a horde of javelina, a side canyon with its adjacent hills and hidden wood, I head down the runnel. My goal for this three-day outing is to walk Hot Springs Canyon to the San Pedro River and explore this perennial stream and its environs.

Arizona-river-walking is always a rewarding experience. The burden of the vertical climb is gone. Less physically taxed you're free to drink in your surroundings.

A light breeze moves through gill-fringed jungle thickets. Autumn leaves dance to the rhythms of its measured motion. I strong-arm my way through willow screens. March through adjacent parks planted in tall grass and stately cottonwood. The canyon cluttered with vegetation, overgrown and gone to seed. A late fall color collage.

One never gets past the novelty of flowing water across a dry land, that this oasis is an apparition and cannot last. To watch and listen to water tumble over a bed of cobblestone is reward enough. But the accord of this landscape's anatomy, the quiver cliffs towering, the bony mountain buttes, the spangling flow of startling stream, the repose of forest, the undisturbed calm in cerulescent skies; the intricate harmony of this rock-ruffian paradise rests heavy on the spirit.

The river flows, and so the miles, and so the afternoon. Saguaros groom the steep grassy hillsides. Cedars tidy the cooler slopes. The last rays of coruscating sunlight ride the tricky mountain skylines and the river bottom grows cold in blue, evening shadows.

On a high sandy beach above the rush of water, under a florescent amethystine sky that must be seen to believed,

I make camp. An almost half moon hangs above the ebony silhouette of incised canyon wall. The white arms of a sycamore canopy the corona of my warming fire. Through the night, the swift brook babbles. Sometimes speaking in distinct sounding syllables and so much like a human voice, I pause to catch the words of someone dithering, only to realize it is just the whirling water. The stars shine, the waters sing, sleep is the easiest thing I've done all day.

With the morning, hoar-frost like a light snow holds everything in its garlanded grip. Climbing several hundred feet of a steep hillside I stand in the warmth of a new day's sun; the land reviles itself an extraordinary work of creation. The Santa Catalina and the Rincon Mountains are bunting-blue walls, worlds away. Below, bubbling quicksilver-waters, cut a canyon through the scone brown hills. Chiseled buttes stand watching a difficult land.

The day's course is without the burden of the backpack. The canyon deepens, the sprite spittle knifing into its perdurable rock bottom, thinning the forest to an occasional tree. I walk where the lion walks. At times the whole floor of the canyon is cut from solid stone where water scoots and scurries along the polished surfaces. On cuddling sandy shores lion tracks are everywhere, in such profusion I expect one to leap into view at any moment. Hawks work the skies. Kingfishers chatter. One gray heron appears. Green finches flit through the willows. Turkey vultures fly and float and decorate the day.

The wayfaring waters of Hot Springs twist and turn, low hills rise from the canyon floor, ceremonious saguaros stare down from the stripped slopes keeping company with bygone baronial grotesquely bent cedars; stone monoliths rise above these to dwarf the occasional gigantic cottonwood.

Afternoon sun finds me resting along saguaro-studded shores. Cottonwood gold glistening on half-clothed branches. Conciliating crystal waters, gurgling.

After logging some miles and with the day wearing down, certain that I am closing in on the San Pedro, I look to climb out of this deepening gulch to gain some perspective. But how far, before I can safely scale the now almost perpendicular walls? A way up and out is found and worth the wait.

Before me is as picturesque a western scene as one might summon by sorcery. The stream below snakes its way through a series of retreating blue ridges that plunge to the canyon bottom, forming a gate to the wide and expanding San Pedro River Valley. This sequence of trailing ethereal blue cutouts forces the eye to the western mountains, their profiles, as a never-resting ocean tossed, but the waves, dyed a deeper blue. Braided silver threads, a river runs. Colossal cottonwoods docked along the stream's edge, dwarfed by swift rising canyon walls. Their golden leaves gleaming in the pure rays of a late afternoon sun.

The vermilion rock ridge I've won, is a desert absolute of cactus and creosote. To the east, rise grassy brass windrows stacked like loaves of French bread to broil and bake in the desert sun thrown as a peck of pillared pickup-sticks at the feet of the titan castle towers of the Galiuros.

With the golden, heaped-up hills that rise before me and the red rock ridge upon which I stand and a hundred shades of creased and crinkled blue corrugations prolonged and preceding into the sun – I am part and parcel of a dreamscape to rival any Georgia O'Keeffe canvas.

A great wind starts to blow and the sun sinks toward the horizon. I must retreat up the canyon and make camp before dark; I'll have to hurry. The sun's last grin probes the canyon hall with its lasers and the wind plays the pass like a pipe organ. A blustery, cold, moonlit night rewards me with two shooting stars.

On the wings of this winnow, a storm approaches. With the dawn, the once cloudless sky now threatens. Dark brooding dims spit rain. Cold, searching winds delve deep the layers of my long johns. I hurry up the canyon to escape impending doom.

After several hours of walking and wading, fighting the raw gale, climbing out of the canyon drift over the last hill past the Muleshoe Ranch house and the percolating hot springs to my waiting truck.

Through the next two days, the storm deposits forty inches of snow in the high country and temperatures plummet – a timely escape.

Arizona is just a pile of rocks, though it be – a beautiful pile of rocks. It cannot be described as a land of promise in the classical sense. It appeals to me on many levels. If beauty, all that could be found here; that would be enough upon which to be content. I'm convinced that there is more to this than meets the eye. That the things placed before us are representative of deeper spiritual realities not always apparent.

If, *"Nature is the Art of God,"* to quote Thomas Browne, then landscape is saturated with spiritual analogy. For what artist worth his salt could be satisfied with painting just the natural objects he sees, in insisting these things portray and delineate the esoteric?

Is it possible to walk across a desert land and upon discovering a seep or a spring or a flowing river and not be impressed by the resonant spiritual implications of such a phenomenon? Not in the trappings themselves, which are wonderful and remarkable, but in what ethereal substance they represent. This celestial component is the ingredient that satisfies and keeps me on the saunter.

And so I gadabout, captivated by the intricate tapestry that is Arizona. I am drawn by the shear weight of its brimful beauty and this tangible, spiritual correspondence, to walk *This Gloryland*: the aesthetically pleasing and comprehensive sweep of this creation; its worthless creosote deserts, the symmetry of its forested mountain skylines, its graceful prairies, its shining rivers. The proportionate arrangement of these contrasting parts. The pleasing impressions of its size, colors and forms have come to rest on my mind like a melody… With a melody in mind.

I rose to a perfect day
The sun it shines on the forests, farms and fields
And as it touched this heart, there's a melody revealed
With a melody in mind.

Hot Springs Canyon,
Galiuro Mountains

Chapter 11:
Far Trails

There are streams that flow
Through blue spruce forests where the lion lay low
Where that creek music plays
And the chirp of the cricket and the songbird
Form a chorusing of praise
That beckon... climb up... climb up... come see
That beckon... come wander... far and free
Find rest on peaks that stand in stars

When deserts smell like rain
When cloud banners christen
This sterile stony greasewood plain
Through the washed atmosphere
Fragrant sun shafts play those water walls
Then rainbows appear
Like angels they've come to set me free
They beckon... come search out this mystery
Well, I can't explain things I don't know... but I must go

"Far trails they're a waitin' on me... valleys vast and still
Vistas undreamed of... fair flowered meadows
Canyon guarded streams... forests enchanted
Filled with magic dreams"

There are streams that flow
Through blue spruce forests where the lion lay low
Where that creek music plays
And the chirp of the cricket and the songbird
Form a chorusing of praise
That beckon... climb up... climb up... come see
That beckon... come wander... far and free
Now, I can't explain things I don't know... but I must go
Far trails.

Chapter 12:
El Rio de San Pedro

*"The waters of the San Pedro were full of fish, large numbers
being taken daily, during our stay on the stream; the hillsides
and the mesas swarmed with quail, rabbits and pheasants.
Bear were frequently seen in the cañon and deer, antelope and
turkeys abound. Extensive forests of cottonwood and
ash lined the river and the adjoining mesas and arroyos were
natural pasture fields for countless herds and flocks."*

– James Leach, 1858

The San Pedro River Valley has a history that is considerably
longer than man's recorded accounts of his own. Emerging
from the shadows of a dreamtime past, people have been
coming and going in this extraordinary watershed, beyond the
comprehendible clasp of ciphering-clock and computation and
the arithmetic of time.

Stone Age Clovis Men, eleven-thousand years ago, were busy
battling Woolly Mammoth and a cold unending. As the
wintery wet weather retreated a hotter and dryer climate
moved across the land; the Cochise Culture arose, latter still,
the Hohokam primed prospered, as generation after
generation farmed irrigated garden plots along the animated
river while hunting deer and antelope.

Centuries chimed, the Spanish arrived, and the narrative
opens as we know it. The narrative we know, is wonderful.

The Spanish conquistador Coronado marched an army down
the river in 1540 in search of *Cibola* and a quick ticket to
fortune and fame. The glories of which they dreamed would
not be realized. The very ground over which they tread
unawares contained the bona fide riches they were looking for
and in time would be revealed to others.

Explorer and missionary Father Kino in 1692 walked the river
in search of souls and a place to build a church.

The Spanish Presidio *"Santa Cruz de Terrenate"* was built in 1775 along the riverbanks. The brutal Apaches were unrelenting and the outpost abandoned.

The San Pedro became a Mexican river in 1821 when they won their independence from Spain and an American river with the Gadsden Purchase in 1853.

The 49ers moved along the watercourse, the only dependable life-saving stream as they fared toward the Gila River on a long arduous journey to California gold.

Edward Schieffelin discovered silver in 1877 and the now infamous town of Tombstone, became the largest city west of St. Louis and east of San Francisco. The windfall opened the floodgates of progress, bringing the railroads, ranchers and miners. The conquest of the American West played out like a Hollywood matinee.

The Apache wars, the cattlemen, the settlers, the prospectors, the shoot-outs and gunfights, the truths, the legends and the lies that we love regarding western American history, unfolded within the valley of the San Pedro. It reads like a dime-store cowboy-novelette. It may be hard to distinguish fact from fiction, the gospel, from what we've seen on the silver screen or read in books, but it really doesn't matter. The west is a place for dreams; it requires it of all its residents and all you've ever heard about the rip-roaring-wild-west, happened right along this consequential conduit the Spanish named *El Rio de San Pedro*.

The Bureau of Land Management has acquired almost forty miles of the river as it flows out of Sonora Mexico on its 140-mile, northward journey through Arizona and established the San Pedro Riparian National Conservation Area. Any stream that flows year-round in Arizona is a big deal. The San Pedro is the largest remaining undammed river in the southwest and an ecological treasure.

The river valley has been described as the biological equivalent of the Grand Canyon. Apparently, more mammals than in any comparable area on the planet, excluding a tropical Costa Rican rainforest. Birds, four-hundred varieties have been tallied; half of all the avian species found in the

United States can be seen flying along the river banks; five-million migrant birds in a typical spring, fourteen-hundred plants and counting. There are mountain lions and bobcats, javelina, gray-fox, deer, coyote, coatimundi, and adorable ringtail cats, all a mix in a zoological-gumbo and seasoned with occasional jaguar. I'm on my way.

The game plan is to walk the river from the international border where it enters Arizona, north to Charleston; about thirty miles. Logistically, just getting there and back will be the hardest part of the trip; not the torrid trek itself. Considering the river's course and the way the roads run, it's easier to thumb my way to the starting point and back home again, than try to rejoin my truck after the expedition's end. The thumb it must be.

The sun poured through my windows bright, like melted butter, as I downed some breakfast and finished stuffing my pack with necessary provisions for the journey. A shot of adrenaline lightened my step as I drifted through the cool morning air and the town of Patagonia. Three blocks through the quiet hamlet, Harshaw Road starts its way through the Patagonia Mountains and the second car sends me flying toward the San Pedro – some forty miles distant.

Three rides transport me across the expansive San Rafael Valley, almost effortlessly, a near miracle. This quintessential cattle and horse country is as imposing as it is exceedingly beautiful and the unpaved roads infrequently traveled. Spacious skies, handsome open oak forests, aureate wide roomy prairies, brazen blue mountains circling where prong-horn antelope stand watching between rides.

With the third spin, I reach the crest of a pass, a notch in the southern end in the aspirant Huachuca Mountains, which partition the valleys of the San Rafael and the San Pedro. From this high vantage point, I can peer deep into Mexico. I can see clearly the San Pedro's graceful course as it slides out of Sonora and starts its long Arizona run, a green serpentine line of behemoth cottonwood timber. A forest fire is burning on one of the Mexican Sierras across the line; smoke pouring off its slopes like a dragster on a quarter-mile run, sending ash plumes miles through the otherwise incandescent atmosphere.

The car practically falls off the juniper-cloaked slopes of near perpendicular walls as we pitch and plunge down the other side of the overlook, working our way off the sylvan inclines and a diminishing mountain. The road straightens out and a broad, grass valley holds sway once more.

This is my stop. My ride heads north. I have a four-mile hike southeast to the river. Gale force winds are whipping across the prairie of gold grass and mesquite and the burning mountain works like a signal-flare, as I hone in on the green line of the river.

About a mile and a half from the river, I reach the international border. A six-foot, steel-wire fence divides the third world from the Promised Land. I take advantage of the patrol road that runs its length and dart down the cleared path for the approaching oasis.

I stop my feet and miss stepping on a huge snake. It's not threatening, though I've never distinguished one like it. Ivory and copper blotched, as long as my six-foot frame, with a fist-sized girth. After a few moments of a kind of stand off, we go our separate and solitary ways.

The keen winds are stoking the raging wildfire so the Mexican Mountains flame like volcanoes. It looks like the last days of Pompei as I slide down the final ridge to the river.

Cottonwoods tower and sing with the wind. Water barely flows across the soft gooey sand packed with tiny minnows. The green grassy shores of the stream fall on the retina with indubitable surprise and delight. Sand-snipes strain to be heard above the rush of air through the trees. I relax for a few moments and drink it all in as I peer down the watercourse with anticipation. I glory in my circumstance.

Water flows in shallow veins across the stream-skids. As I walk along, snipes run candid to announce my presence on the river. The banks of the runnel are low and beyond the cottonwood margins, the aloof Huachuca and Mule Mountains can be seen protecting the valley's perimeters. Inescapable the bold bright sun; the landscape awash under its intense radiative beams, reveals the San Pedro's thin flowing necklaces of liquid diamonds.

On a May afternoon like this one, 449 years ago, Francisco Vasquez de Coronado is leading an army down this river in search of Cibola. It is the largest exploratory endeavor assembled in the Americas; 250 horsemen, 70 foot soldiers,1,300 Indians, 1,000 horses, 500 pack animals, herds of cattle and sheep. This is serious business. They'll go on to explore Arizona, New Mexico, even Kansas, only to return, stone-broke and starving. On a May afternoon like this one, 449 years ago.

Unlike the Spanish, I will find the troves and treasures I chase.

To my surprise, after some two mileposts, the river sinks right into the sand. The watercourse that held such promise dries up completely. After filling up my canteens with the last of it, I traipse what seems like mile after mile of a waterless stream. Walking is difficult in the dune soft sand and not at all fun with the weight of my pack. Drained and dispirited, tried in the trick and tomfoolery. Have I come this far, to struggle down a crackling, dry creek? A river without water is hardly a river at all.

The day draws to a close. Climbing up a sandy bank, I pitch the tent and work on freeze-dried sweet and sour pork, swatting mosquitoes between bites. The glory sun sinks behind baronial blue-walls of the Huachuca Mountains, leaving the land under a half moon's milky light. I'm very tired, just wanting to lie down and close my eyes.

"A city set upon a hill cannot be hid." The Mexican Sierras brightly blaze through the night like some grand civilization in apocalyptic collapse.

On an evening like this one, 112 years ago, prospector Edward Schieffelin is looking for some color in the local hills. Tonight he's feeling lucky, but he won't spark up a fire for fear of marauding Apaches. On an evening like this one, 112 years ago.

With the morning, the old-world is a brand-new-world, embroidered wide and fair before me; and will be. I break camp and step back into the dried-up river. A quarter mile, the water springs forth from the desert sands. Back in business.

Indescribable, the appealing allure of the river, a puissant-palette of complementary colors these early morning hours.

The cool shadowy canopy created by the protective cotton-wood. Dazzling sunbeams pierce the green-leafed roof and play on the sparkling flow of water, like spotlights on a country singers sequined suit. Striking vivid greens, brilliant against the blue sky. The atmosphere, flawlessly clear, to match the lucid-liquid at my feet, pungent with the perfumes of a world boundlessly alive. El Rio de San Pedro: an animate, watery, sylvan tunnel, across a gold-bullion grass ocean.

Water flows over a flat bed of soft sand perhaps thirty-feet wide. Shallow silverware channels weave their way back and forth across the slightly-tilted table as it rolls down long sheltered corridors built of stately cottonwood collars. Little tadpoles and minnows in countless numbers are packed into every available drop of water.

I am not a birder, nor a likely ornithologist. It matters far less to me what they are, but that they are. It's no wonder enthusiasts come from far and wide to see what flies and funnels through this valley. The obvious vermilion flycatcher, and a blue bunting. There are jeweled hummingbirds, orioles, cardinals, green, gray and yellow finches and sparrows and a summer tanager. There are kingfishers and falcons, Harris hawks and redtails. Egrets and great gray herons lift gracefully off the water with each bend in the river. Brown ducks quack above the trees, while mothers with the broken-wing routine, try and divert my attention, as the little ones run for their lives. Snipes or perhaps some kind of plover continually walk in front of me with an unending peep… peep… peeping.

It's a lot of fun walking a river like this. The sense of wonder and discovery never dissipates. Each bend has its own temperament. It is with joyous anticipation I peek around each sinuous turnstile to see how the witching-waterway presents itself anew.

On a morning like this one, twelve-hundred years ago, Hohokam women are irrigating small plots of corn and beans. Men are out hunting for dinner and deer in downy-tracts of prairie. Children are playing in the restless waters wandering, on a marvelous morning like this one, twelve-hundred years ago.

The San Pedro gains a slight increase in its volume of water. Sometimes it's a babbling brook, or a river forty-five feet wide, three and a half deep. But more often, its languid and sluggish flow slinks like a snake over a wide, sandy bed. Surpassingly picturesque, the run reminds me of Neshaminy Creek, a stream I knew well as a boy, back in Pennsylvania; then again, it isn't like that at all. Often reminiscent of some color canvas fashioned by a "Hudson River School Painter" of the 1800s, on the American wilderness. Stately tall trees reflected in tranquil waters cast a Victorian shadow across a land, wild and untamed.

On a May morning like this one in 1852, A.B. Clarke, bound for California gold, moved down this section of the San Pedro. Three men in his party attacked a grizzly bear. They dropped him three times, but the creature kept coming. With the bear very near, and with the last load of buckshot, they let it fly into the face of a beast gone ballistic. They all ran – the bear in one direction, the men in the other. That was the last they saw of the marauding monster. The river is not so wild these days, but it's a comfort to know that lions still prowl these sheltered shores, and infrequent jaguar, not an impossibility.

"The road is pretty good down this splendid valley
although in some places rather rough,
trees are becoming common on the river;
its direction is indicated by them for a long distance.
They are principally cottonwoods,
with some sycamore, willow and mesquite.
A fawn was brought into camp in the evening."

On May evenings and mornings, like this one, 136 years ago.

The river is mine alone. I can climb the banks and see ranches in the distance and there are at times fields quite close, but on the whole, the river seems left unto itself and me with it. The day is a series of enchanted landscape paintings. I strain to make mental notes on each bend and bow of the river, hoping to remember it all, an unattainable pant.

Turn after turn and stretch after stretch the river flows, mile after mile the powder dry shores don't drink it dry. I keep expecting this to happen. It has not rained one inch on this valley in four months. The sun, any day, everyday, unrelenting, beats down on this vale. How does the river proceed?

The real question is – will this endangered river keep trickling in the years to come? Sadly, ninety percent of the free-flowing streams in southern Arizona have disappeared due to man's exploitation of the ground water. Killing the living waters and taking with it all the extraordinary life dependent on it. Sierra Vista, a small but fast growing city on the shoulders of this valley, threatens to do the same here. I pray that won't ever happen, for that my good friend; would be nothing short of sin.

Great dehydrated-tributaries enter the San Pedro at different intervals, having run for miles across the broad arid valley they give up their bounty to the river's increase. Though these big wadis are bone dry at the moment, when running, have the potential to magnify the water-flow in alarming proportions.

I met a man with a story to tell. Picnicking with his family on the San Pedro some forty miles down stream, an outrageous flash flood came upon them. A mad rushing wave of water, with trees being turned end over end, like acrobatic tumblers, ranted and raced down the river. Scrambling up the river walls, they escaped just in time with their lives. Such dangers do not exist for me today and it's hard to believe that they ever could, as I wander mile after mile down this placid and peaceful stream.

I startle some resting deer in a thicket of cottonwood and like an exploding grenade they fly in all directions. Though one lingers, perhaps to see if I might give chase. I assure him that can't happen carrying this weighty pack. Not being completely convinced, he vanishes with two bounding leaps – gone.

On a morning like this one, 129 years ago, Cochise and a raiding party of twenty are returning with some stolen horses from Sonora. They will stop here for a drink before bolting across the desert and disappearing into their Dragoon Mountain Stronghold. On a morning like this one, 129 years ago.

Big frogs jump and plop in the water at my approach, they're so fast, I never see them. But not in any number to match the prolific quantity of tadpoles in the water which, without exaggeration must rank in the billions. A discovery is made.

Resting on a grassy bank watching the water flow, I come to realize I'm not alone. At once, the very ground on which I sit is alive with tiny little toads, the size of my thumbnail. In unfathomable numbers, like a locust plague, the ground writhes in frolicking frog-flesh. It is nothing short of fantastic. I assume the healthy population of herons must be gorging themselves on these miniature amphibians. If you're a lover of frog's legs, it's a glutton's delight.

The river is a beguiling, green serpent, the enticing terrain through which it flows. The majesty of the mountains blue, the valley's sweep of gold grass, the green string of cottonwood pearls, which is the river's bounty. The accord of these component parts that form this landscape and the amaranthine life upon it; these things attest to God's glory. Though I am a man like any other, I feel closest to Him on these excursions. Perhaps this walking and my wonder-filled gaze, my best form of worship.

"Varied forms, high and low, are simply portions of God radiated from Him as a sun and made terrestrial by the clothes they wear, and by the modifications of a corresponding kind in the God essence itself."

– John Muir

On a glorious day like today, 230 years ago, Father Kino, under a broad-brimmed hat, is moving down the river. He's looking for converts and possible mission sites. He's making a map of the river's course, noting the position of the mountains. He's making friends, on a glorious day like today, 230 years ago.

There are roads that bridge the river. I know the fourth one will be the road that leads me back to civilization. At the close of the day, having passed the third bridge by a good distance and being very tired, I look for an appropriate campsite for the night. It's been a remunerative day.

Walking up a waterless draw just off the river, I come face to face with a doe reclined on a bank and nestled in the woven-weaves of tangled grass. Turning my head for just a moment, as I set down my pack, I look up to find her gone.

The soft sand makes excellent bedding for my tent and I look forward to sleep. But not before the distant dimming blue cants of the Huachuca Mountains are painted lavender and vermilion ribbons of smoke from the still-flaming Mexican forest fire, flag against a burnished copper sky and the sun calls it another day.

El Rio de San Pedro

On an evening like this one, though probably colder, eleven-thousand years ago, stone age Clovis Men have killed a mastodon on the haggard hills that rise up before me. There is celebration and good eating. The bones and stone projectiles that they have used to slay the unreasoning brute will be found by modern man, on these very hills, on an evening like this one, eleven-thousand years ago.

Morning temperatures are cold and after breakfast I scrape off the ice from my formerly soggy sneakers and step back into the e'lan river. With the first three steps, a great blue heron lifts off the water. The curtain rises, yesterday's theater presentation a reprise, variations on a theme.

The headliners are the ducks. Sometimes bursting off the water in bundles of fifteen, but more often, in coveys of four or five and winging over the cottonwood with surprising speed. Lots of herons and egrets, a very large black snake and a cameo appearance of a strange and extraordinary hawk, the likes of which, I have never seen. (It's a "Mexican eagle" of the flag of Mexico, the crested caracara. The Mexican peso coin shows the caracara hacking a wriggling rattlesnake to death with its beak.) The sighting of six javelina, one desert-fox, three coyotes, and four, vaulting deer completes the im-promptu ensemble.

It is a handsome river and each turn proves it. The morning unfolds like the day before, with sovereign stretch and strain reiterated, the river unwinds.

I've dropped in elevation since the river's start and the grass-lands have given way to barbed-brambles and creosote seas. After a few miles, low desert hills move in close and it is apparent there's a harsh reality beyond this green oasis.

I pray this paradise goes on forever. But another world, regret-fully, does exist beyond this river. After a morning march of six miles, I arrive at the fourth bridge and the ghost town of Charleston.

On a morning like this one, one-hundred years ago, wagons shuttle silver ore down from the hills of Tombstone for processing mills along the river. Charleston is one swingin' community. It goes on all night long. There is a continuous flux of miners, prospectors, gamblers, cowboys, ladies of the night and of course, occasional gunfights. Doc Holliday and Wyatt Earp are sleeping in. Up early, and up to no good, Curly Bill Brosious and Johnny Ringo, on a morning like this one, one-hundred years ago.

The San Pedro will run another hundred miles north emptying its waters into the Gila River and in turn, the Colorado, then, hobbling on to the Gulf of California. Though these days except for floods, the desert sands drink the waters dry a handful of miles ahead. To that demarcation, the river remains government protected, but presently, it's closed to the public. This is as far as I go: twelve-noon.

Just off a quiet country bridge, I stick out my thumb. Three rides transport me back to Patagonia and by 2:00 P.M., I'm sitting on the porch of my humble abode. I cannot be certain I've just awakened from a dream or that all this has actually gone down as stated. Though my soggy shoes and muddy pants attest clear evidence that an engaging ancient river still runs down a grand sweep of valley, and I trust will continue to do so – for the next ten-thousand years

"To speak of sparing anything because it is beautiful
is to waste one's breath and incur ridicule in the bargain."

– John C. Van Dyke

The San Pedro River and this valley are remarkable. The Nature Conservancy, when looking around the country and assessing ecosystems worthy of protection, puts this valley in the top five.

Along its journey from here to the Gila River, there are a few places where water springs from the desert sands and flows for a few miles along the surface. The resulting oasis is nothing short of miracles and magic. There is a portion nigh St. David and Cascabel, another east of San Manuel, and a good segment north of Winkelman.

In the years to come, I will buy a home in San Manuel and will spend more than a decade wandering every tributary canyon, every mountain range rimming the long-spun valley. Logging hundreds of river miles. Walking its verdant course and exploring the exceptional deserts that border this singularly stunning stream. I consider these patent places my own personal property.

Just the Galiuro Mountains east of San Manuel has a block of wily wilderness worthy of national monument status, but of course this is the last thing I would propose for such a wonderful place. But it is not hyperbole to pronounce. It is only a measure as to how much I think these natural resources are worth – the seven perennial streams the Galiuros contribute to the San Pedro watershed and, of course, the glory of Aravaipa Canyon.

Buehman Creek, the only living stream on the eastern face of the Santa Catalina Mountains that enters the San Pedro in the same general area, has been a source of spiritual and photographic inspiration for years, an image I share in this book.

One of the lurking luxuries of residing here – I live in a huge empty unpeopled valley, with abandoned, bountiful blocks of wilderness. Even if you don't go in, it's nice to know it's there. Isn't that why we have all moved to the southwest? It can't be just because it's sunny. It is these oversized, open spaces, which set our souls free and our hearts to flutter. But a desert is just a desert until you find a magical stream flowing across it.

We have all come from somewhere else to fill the Arizona wilderness with an ugly city. If we drink these waters dry and kill the very thing we have come here to love, we will have shown ourselves very poor stewards.

Ecological issues, for me, are a crashing bore and like theology, no one can agree on anything. This incessant bickering leaves me weary in spirit. It makes me want to throw up my hands and take a walk somewhere. If there was ever a place worthy of our concern and protection, it is these tributary streams and this dreamlike beautiful river.

Dreams are like rivers that flow through your mind
With their banks filled with rain… but, you haven't the time
To catch half of those thoughts as they're drifting on by
Though they glimmer and shine as the river unwinds.

"Coyote is always out there, and he is always hungry."

– Tony Hillerman

Chapter 13:
Hilltops High and Fair

It is well to live in the valley sweet
Where the work of the world is done
Where the reapers sing in the fields of wheat
As they toil beneath the setting sun
But beyond these meadows the hills I see
Where the noise and the traffic cease
And I follow a voice that calleth to me
From the hilltop regions of peace

There are mountains that wait
Beyond these city gates
To the hilltops high and fair

To live is sweet in the valley fair
And to toil beneath the setting sun
But my spirit yearns for the hilltop's air
When the day and its work are done
For a presence breathes o'er those silent hills
And its sweetness is living yet
The same deep calm all the hillsides fill
As breathed over Olivet

There are mountains that wait
Beyond these city gates
To the hilltops high and fair... and there
God's finest whispers to hear
In bright streams running clear
On those hilltops high and fair

It is well to live in the valley sweet
Where the work of the world is done.

The Grassy Ridge -
The Galiuro Mountains

Chapter 14:
The Grassy Ridge

"Plants and animals change as one goes up the mountain,
and so apparently, do people."

– Diana Kappel-Smith / *Desert Time*

The Galiuro Mountains are the scenic backdrop from my residence in San Manuel. From my windows an unending color show holds my attention and continues to deepen my appreciation for this range set apart.

In the blue shadows of morning, the Sierra is a cardboard cutout, a waving line of indigo. Afternoons flood its contours with light and define them for what they are, a bad-ass crumple of rocky ridges struggling to support a forest of oak and piñon pine on its heightened crowns. At its feet a flowing apron of stony slopes filled with saguaros and creosote that collar the mountains, forming a wide waterless protective perimeter.

Multiplicities and impediments leap from the ground like Everest when cumulus, troop. On cloudless days when washed of color, the lashings are small in stature, cabalistic, velvetized and dreamy in a storm. With the glory fires of evening, molten canyons anvil out the final shapes of another magnificent day. Sunset mountaintops glow fluorescent lavender under a desert moon.

Dr. Hendrickson owns the ranch and works the range below the Grassy Ridge. He is kind enough to unlock a ranch road gate, letting me gain access to YLE canyon and unexplored territory.

I leave the ranch house behind. The rough road winding through several small canyons, climbing the gradual grades choked with cactus, creosote, and occasional cows. Not far from a stock tank and gyrating windmill, I park the truck and I'm on my way.

YLE starts out with a wide rocky floor and low ranking saguaro filled hills. The imposing blue wall of the Galiuros, a few miles distant. Sunny and warm, though clouds are building as I press through a jungle of mesquite and thorny brush near impenetrable. I bob and weave but can't escape the clawing at my pack and the tearing of pant legs as I labor over corpulent cobblestone.

A small mountain runs parallel to the main ridge creating a small valley from which YLE drains. I make a sharp right and move up the draw; saguaros give way to accomplished assemblies of Emory oak and open grassy slopes.

There is a raw edge to the look of these rambunctious mountains that is unnerving, uncultivated and unkempt. The landscape looks like a scene from a Hobbit novel, should some hobgoblin leap from the bush. Gnarled dwarfed oaks no bigger than men crouching in the corners. A lingering loneliness about the place and yet contradictorily congenial. In several places, water springs from the ground and the stream runs for a short while on the surface, extravagant rugs of grass and flower. Deer-grazing green lawns beneath the trees. The sun playing the field.

By the time I've logged a few miles, the clouds have turned to thunderhead and brought a light rain as the little valley ends where the small mountain hitches onto the big one. A sharp left turn and two-thousand feet, plus a little bit more, aspires The Grassy Ridge.

Rain ends with a sun shower as I stand on a grass and mesquite terrace above the drainage. Brilliant sun, silver sheets of rain, deer running for their lives.

I advance with the lumbering pace of lead-footed deep sea diver. The afternoon is moving faster than I, with this rough and tumble landscape straight up and down. Cool stiff winds ascending the ridge. It's partly sunny, but I'm often beneath cloud shadows. I'm sweaty, chilled and working hard. My heart pounds like a locomotive and muscles strain against slopes unforgiving. I believe I can muster the physical strength to climb these mountains, but this stifling topography extinguishes the will.

The trail barely discernible as it zigzags over rocky ledges, then a steep spiraling stair, as I follow above a drainage that is carving a deep seam in the mountainside. Upward to a small landing, the trail disappears completely. I can't tell where to go, but the only way is up, almost perpendicular now.

There is nothing but gold grass and the wind. Higher still, to a shelf where woodlands of pine, cedar and oak, make a sudden resolute stand against a determined sun. I drop my pack and walk to the edge of the earth.

Kielberg Canyon plunges into an abyss two-thousand feet deep, a narrow defile separating The Grassy Ridge and the massive stone-burg, Kielberg Peak. In its shadowed facets, a forest of cypress, clinging to slopes that free fall from seven-thousand feet.

The trail leads up a mild incline to a wooded saddle. Then the final six-hundred-foot assault. The path is not clear, but it's up hill from here. A dense forest of stunted oak, not much bigger than myself, clutters the swelling hillsides. I puzzle over the terse trail, pushing my way to the top of the mountain, reaching a brassy grass plateau with well-spaced alligator juniper trees and walking to the opposite edge of the mesa for a marvelous view.

Loosely defined the Galiuros are two great parallel rifts; having reached the top of the first, a panorama of mountain ridge and valley unfurls. A blue wall of seven-thousand foot peaks tumble into Rattlesnake, a gigantic canyon draining half the ragged range. Forests of Douglas fir and Arizona cypress clinging to shaded warn-weary nooks and working down the felling siphons. A ridge flowing off my mountain drops into the valley below partitioning the Kielberg basin, a huge forested bowl that punches through the Galiuros western walls with a frightening gash. Kielberg Mountain is a blue Gibraltar, cut like crystal, catching the flaxen flares of an exiting sun.

The Galiuro Mountains are long and lonesome and derelict of any methodical topography. A countenance of chaos on the Arizona landscape. But there on The Grassy Ridge the mountains make sense. There is balance and symmetry to distempered disorder; one of southern Arizona's best views.

I pitch a tent underneath the outstretched arms of a jibing juniper, five-hundred years old if it's a day. Pleasant evening, mild temperatures, a fragrant fire of cedar, a billion stars.

The most comfortable night's sleep I can ever remember in the wilderness. With the morning glorious sunshine, gold grass, blue mountains.

Don't know where I'm going, so before I break camp, I do some exploring. The Grassy Ridge is a wonderful formation, shaped like a loaf of bread, steep-sided, rounded, flat top. The southern end, where it tumbles into Canyon Kielberg is broad and wide, but the ridge as it travels north, tapers at first slowly, then pinches into a narrow wooded blade. To the west, it drops off precipitously, twenty-five-hundred feet to the desert floor. The top of the table is slightly tilted to the east and at its edges, drops off sharply, but cursively into forested canyons.

One aspen tree growing just below the western lip of the plateau, on a small talused slope, standing in the shade amidst a forest of pygmy piñon pine. You have to walk this land to appreciate its nuance. There is not a hundred aspens growing on this whole mountain range and none on western walls. This is the last tree, in a stand of trees, grown here for ten-thousand years. A youngster, growing up beside it, had not survived. Perhaps too hot and dry now for this tree, even to reproduce. It is the last of the Mohicans and a thousand generations.

Centuries long past, Douglas fir forests filled this plateau and groves of aspen gloried in unseen autumns. Over time, the sun chased the trees into the shadows and determined aspens should disappear completely, except for one. Perhaps this blistering Sonoran-sun shall retreat and cooler seasons bequeath the former woodlands. But I'm betting that won't happen anytime soon and witness the end of an age.

I find the trail I'm looking for, walk back across the plateau, dismantle camp and down I go.

A streamer of trees flows off The Grassy Ridge declining into the central canyons and a clear trail leads the way. I drop a thousand feet with glimpses into Rattlesnake Canyon and unobstructed views into the font of Kielberg as The Grassy Ridge rises behind me, more like a leavened loaf.

At the bottom of the wrinkle I park my pack. Drop off the saddle into Kielberg basin to visit Power's Mine and then into the depths of the bowl.

The small valley is a hallowed pocket where stands of ancient cypress cast a primeval spell. At the headwaters, a quiet brook tumbles through a deepening ravine to carve a wicked-wedge between Kielberg Mountain and The Grassy Ridge and a colossal canyon. I don't know just how far this clove can be traversed but one thing is for certain, no one ever goes down there – not ever. Back up the saddle to my pack and lunch.

In 1909, Jeff Power and his family began homesteading in the Galiuro Mountains and commenced working a claim on the ridge just below me. They had gumption and enterprise, building a road twenty miles from the tiny town of Klondike, through lonesome Rattlesnake Canyon, up and over this furrow and fold where I sit.

They brought in equipment to work the mine, an ore-crusher farther down the canyon and built a house called Powers Garden. Capital layout had to be substantial. I have little faith that they could have gleaned enough treasure to make it worth their hard-while or mustered the strength to accomplish the building of a dream, which, in the end, brought tragedy.

The Powers weren't winning any popularity contests back in Klondike. When Jeff's sons didn't volunteer to fight the war to end all wars and answer as conscripts for military service, a letter arrived, asking them to come in and threatening prosecution. It was ignored. They sent out a posse.

On February 9, 1918, Deputy U.S. Marshal Frank Haynes, Sheriff Robert F. McBride of Graham County, and Deputy Sheriffs Martin Kempton and T.K. Wooten, crept up the canyon through the numb of night. Arriving at the Powers cabin near the mine, they lay in wait with arrest warrants in hand for Tom and John for draft evasion. Jeff Power and his hired man Tom Sisson were wanted on unrelated charges. Pandemonium, default, death and dying came with the dawn.

After a fast and furious gunfight, Kempton, McBride and Wooten where obsolete, as well as Powers Senior. Haynes was high-tailing it back to Klondike. Brothers and hired hands were on the run to Redington and the San Pedro River and for borders beyond and Arizona's largest manhunt was set in motion.

Their crime was probably more self defense then offense. The authorities came in shooting. The Powers shot back. Though the truth will never be known, Tom Sisson died in prison and the Power boys spent most of the rest of their lives in jail.

After lunch, I march down the switch-back road that Powers built and drop into Rattlesnake Canyon. I make camp where the primitive path meets the pour and spend the rest of the afternoon walking toward Powers Garden.

Lots of good water tumbles down the stream-cobblestones and the wide flat canyon floor is filled with handsome ponderosa, skeletal sycamore and the regal oak. These woodlands are planted like a garden. I marvel to think that with a random throw of seeds a timber stand could raise itself with such esthetics. That mile after mile it should go on this way. That this much especial space could still be untouched.

For diversion, I wander up Corral Canyon heading east. Very clear tracks in the sand. Lions and bears, oh my! I press on, hoping to get lucky. I run out of gas.

There's no shortage of unruly critters wandering these jungles. But try and catch some gallivanting apart from the blue flash of a racketing Mexican Jay. A herd of elephants could be interspersed in this touting tangle of trees and remain undetected. Though walking long corridors, omnibus-albums respecting gallant groves, the plum and the prize: these wild woods make known what lonesome is and how lonesome it can be.

I return to camp an hour before it grows dark. I prepare for a cold night. Deer in the shadows as I gather wood.

Thank God for long johns and a fire; without such luxuries this explorer would perish. I cuddle the flames like a lover. Beyond the fires glow, it's an icebox. My breath, a long smoky column. Through the pine canopy's open windows, a billion stars cannot warm the arctic ebony hours. A cold night in a cold bag is in small measure, eternity.

Slow to rise, for the morning is as frigid as the night. After breakfast, I head up Rattlesnake for the most edifying part of my peregrinations.

Rattlesnake Canyon starts its lengthy run by tumbling off the western face of the eastern rift of the Galiuros, then turning to scamper and scurry between the mountain chain's parallel ridges. The canyon gradually climbing up the mountainsides, the walls closing in, being more shaded by topography, where a marvelous Canadian forest resides.

These mountains are filled with curious sequestered niches where biologic communities have survived by caprice of sun and shadow. What makes them matchless and magical, higher still, on mountain-sheathes that carry the weight of a summer sun, nothing more than stunted cedar and agave and the chaotic mishmash of manzanita, can summon an appeal.

Along the cool canyon bottom old growth stands of daunting Douglas fir, parliaments of pillared ponderosa, crocheted congregations of Arizona cypress, bringing a cathedral silence and majesty, with understories of dead fern and leafless maples and a handful of aspens that shouldn't be there.

A divine composition of rock wood and water, cherubic-rhapsody and rhetoric; this walk of a few miles is an act of worship, done with reverence and awe, with a joyful exuberance. If heaven more handsome, we're in for a treat. Though best to visit in summer when bears roam, or fall when these marvelous maples set the forest to fire with color. Any season, every man a believer. For in such exultant beauty, does God not have His hand in?

"Everything we see, touch, smell, everything from the sun to a grain of sand, from our own body with its admirable organs, to that of the worm, everything has flowed forth, by a supreme reason, from that world where all is spirit and life."

"The visible creation then, cannot, must not... be anything but the exterior circumference of the invisible and metaphysical world."
– Guillaume Oegger / *The True Messiah*

Humbled by immense timber I browse the sylvan galleries
climbing to the head of the ravine and dropping over the top
of the ridge where Redfield Canyon starts its extended run.
I peer down the somber gorge, which drains the southern half
of this cogent, carefree wilderness. Paradoxically, there is a
singular melancholy possessing the manor that spies and
spooks these talismanic sculpt-clefts and hauntingly cuts to
the core. Solitary and estranged intendment – a fallen and feral
look to the place that leaves my spirit perfectly unsettled.
A trail should lead the way, but it's completely overgrown.
I turn back for camp, to wander again, the garden alone.
(Whether dead or alive, bears occasionally eat lions here.
I find some scat with embedded lion claw.)

Despite the affectionate lights filtering through the canopy,
I can still discern a hint of my breath in the lingering cool of
this canyon bottom. Another cold night does not appeal.
I head for The Grassy Ridge in hopes of spending the night in
a more temperate location.

Under a warm brilliant sun, up the switchback road to the
top of the saddle, leaving the ponderosa and Douglas fir, up
the blue ramp through thickets of oak and juniper – a pleasant
climb to a waiting plateau which takes most of the afternoon.

I reach the summits, growing more appreciative of loaves, and
of leaven, and of mountain-rise. A retreating sun, washing
over the tilted grass table and golden waves of grain marching
in lockstep with the breezes blowing. Far below Kielberg and
Rattlesnake is the eastern Galiurion rift, tumbling blue
canyons and startling blue mountains; the great blue outback.

Make camp under the outstretched arms of a welcoming
friend. Gathering fragrant cedar to warm the night and spend
the day's last light taking photographs and staring into the
plummeting blue dim depths and the cleavages of Kielberg.

My kingdom for a fire, the black night all stars, very cold.
Warm with the morning sun, blinding light, bleached blond
fields; the blue dollops are cedars, a blue clarion air.

I make a dash across the plateau, north along the narrowing,
roof ridge. From the crest of its wooded blade the derelict,
wide-woebegone valley of the San Pedro River is airbrushed a

spring green. The long gorge of Rattlesnake where tall timber strain the rays of the morning sun.

There's crackling in the woods. For a moment, I exult in the presence of the bear. He worries over mine, throwing himself off the precipitous mountainside into a labyrinth of manzanita as tightly woven as my shirt. Gone.

This beleaguered scrub does not strike me as good bear habitat. I'm wrong. Come summer they're busy here; droppings everywhere.

On the way back, I find an interesting rock that looks almost like opal. Wait a minute; it actually is opal.

After lunch, I start a slow descent for the desert and home. With measured steps, I lower myself down the falling mountainsides, growing warmer by degrees in elevation. Down through the stunted oak and piñon pine. Down the plunging grass slopes to the head waters of YLE canyon.

On the small mesquite terrace above the drainage where I stood in a gleaming sun shower three days before, I startle a drove of deer. With much snorting and grunting, eight charge up and over a small mountain in minutes that would take me an hour to climb.

An eighty-degree spring day in the desert – winter rains have produced verdant lawns where deer find good grazing. I saw only four in the high country, but it will soon warm there as well, renewing mountain meadows and summoning these herds to fill the forests with their delicate presence.

There is elation in fatigue and triumph having gone the distance, with more miles to tread through YLE. Past the Hobbit oak groves and the short runs of flowing stream. Past the green grass rugs, where more deer dart. On through the ocotillo, the cholla, and the prickly pear. Come the saguaros and the bright brittlebush blooms and all the desert hillsides. The final round, wrestling an apostatized wilderness of thorny mesquite to my truck.

The always-brown desert is green and yellow. Late sun, washing the rocky faces of Sombrero Butte, Rhodes Peak, The Grassy Ridge. The truck climbs through the long dissolute canyons, across the broad benches, down the pleated rock aprons to the San Pedro's riverine cottonwood, the Hendrickson Ranch; the end of adventure.

Something happens to the spirit when it tests itself against mountains and revelation at its culmination.

Deeper than canyons, older than mountains, I would that I had wings.

At night before sleep finds me, I fly over desert canyons to a lone aspen on a distant slope. Over blue-forested mountains, into the depths of lonesome canyons, to light by streams beneath whispering fir canopies, finding a rest and joy in the work of His hands, and a peace beyond this beauty, deeper than canyons, older than mountains.

I would that I had wings.

*I find great joy
in simple things,
the hymns of praise
that nature sings,
those intent on listening
confirm the unimproved
works of the Lord.*

Chapter 15:
Patagonia

Left a girl in Patagonia
Her pretty eyes I'll wait to see
I've gone down to Mexico
She waits there for me

Left my dreams in Patagonia
On a ranch in grassy seas
By the trees she kisses deep
And waves goodbye to me

Through the sun and the rain I'll ride
Search some canyon there and hide
A woman cries… and a posse rides
And the town folks choose their sides
In Patagonia

A man could die in Patagonia
In a stupid test of foolish pride
The shot rang out, the bullet deep
A man takes off and rides

Left my dreams in Patagonia
A sweeter love they'll never be
I've gone down to Mexico
She waits there for me in Patagonia Patagonia… Patagonia.

Chapter 16:
Blue On Blue

*"Earth's crammed with heaven and every common bush
afire with God; but only he who sees, takes off his shoes."*

– Elizabeth Barrett Browning

Arizona is a big place. It is not unusual to pilot your vehicle a hundred plus miles, climb up some abandoned canyon, log ten or twelve miles, jump back in the truck and be home in time for dinner. I'm on my way.

I climb out of the Sonoran Desert and the Tucson valley, leaving behind a city too big with its urban clutter, its cactus and creosote wastes, sailing east and south across a vast inland ocean of grass; the plains of Sonoita. Blue mountains fencing a golden sea. Southward to the small settlement of Sonoita and the Canelo Hills beyond, where ghost towns lay interned in the folds of its undulating ridges of oak. Now southeast to my objective, forested foothills crash like elongated indigo waves against the still, distant foundations and impressive 9,400-foot Huachuca summits; there hidden ranches harbor as heavens in narrow grass valleys between the crests of rolling swell. To the south sweep crisp vistas, the San Rafael grasslands reaching deep into Mexico. The purple profiles of the Sierra Madre held in check by this one-hundred-thirty square-mile patch of grass and the blue barricade of the Patagonia Mountains stand to the west. I wend east to the base of the mountain where the road ends and a stream running clear as common sense gushes from the highlands. I strike out on foot.

By any one's calibration, this is gorgeous country. A western scene as visually captivating as any muralist might hope to conjure; big skies, handsome open oak forests, capacious prairies and blue mountains of fir in which to fence it all in. It's been this good looking for some time.

War ended in 1849 with a coerced concord insisting Mexico

relinquish her northern holdings to the United States for the pittance of fifteen-million dollars in reparations. A treaty necessitated a boundary survey commissioned to draw some lines and check out new acquisitions.

Rhode Islander, John Bartlett and head of the project, crossed over the Canelo Hills in September of 1851 to gaze upon the stunning San Rafael Valley and made this note of it.

> *"A few miles brought us to the puerta, or gate in the mountain;*
> *passing which, we emerged into a very broad and*
> *open plain of remarkable beauty.*
> *From the elevation where we first saw this valley,*
> *the prospect was exceedingly picturesque.*
> *Around us grew the maguey, the yucca, and various kinds of cacti,*
> *together with small oaks; while beneath us, the valley spread out*
> *from six-eight miles in width, and some twelve or fifteen in length.*
> *Unlike the desolate and barren plains between the mountain ridges,*
> *which we had crossed between the Rio Grande*
> *and the San Pedro rivers, this valley was covered with*
> *the most luxuriant herbage and thickly-studded with live oaks;*
> *not like a forest, but rather resembling a cultivated park.*
> *While the train was passing down the mountain,*
> *I stopped with Mr. Pratt to enjoy the scene,*
> *which he hastily transferred to his sketch book."*

Some things, fortunately, never change.

Forests of oak and alligator juniper dress the mountainsides in wonderful shades of blue. The canyon stream cutting a trench deep where sycamore and cottonwood find themselves a home beside green grassy lawns and the babble of tumbling waters. I climb up an alluvial fan of rock that has slipped off the hastening mountain slopes like a glacial ice. The creek and the moraine leading to a pine-filled basin where the small conifers are wedged into the dwarfed woodland, though gaining in number and size where shadowy hillsides protect them from the sun. I ladder a few fences and pass a long-abandoned homestead complete with a flowering apple orchard of three trees that stand as ten-foot bouquets. Lion tracks cast in the mud by a broken corral. A huge antlered white-tailed buck melts into the curtains of jungle growth that breathe with the winds massaging blue hillsides. What a country!

A foot trail scales the steep mountain. I climb the ridge like a staircase leaving behind the creek drainage to drift below like a waving blue streamer of crepe paper. With the exception of the crinkle on which I labor, the whole southern exposed face of the mountain is near treeless. Though a few isolated firs topple from dizzying snow-filled crowns.

I discover a mine along the way. Enterprising prospectors managed to drag a Model-T Ford up the slopes. Its engine working the gears and cables to biopsy copper and silver deposits deep within the mountain. A wheel-less chassis remains; its hooded motor, a rusty gearshift pointing skyward, a testimony to man's temporal passing. Despite the crude surgery, the mountain is no worse for the wear.

The ascent continues. A startled drove of deer plumb the falling cant. Jet-black ravens and red-tailed hawks drift overhead. A teasing wind steals my hat to leave me chasing felted quarry and its cutting cold welcomes me to the high country. Green moss mats the forest floor. Bear scat; evidence of summer feasting. Snow melt rivulets, weave through mingling crowds of Douglas fir tattling. A timberland primeval but too cold to stay, though I press to the summit stones. To the east the San Pedro Valley and the wispy strands of cottonwood forestry that garnish the rivers long run – the incurious Mule Mountains. The snowy pyramid of the Santa Ritas stand to the north. Most of a hundred air miles to the west, Boboquivari's blue finger.

The language of landscape beautifully composed. A fretted surface of blue ridges punctuated by gold grass. Silver cirrus stall over snow-capped peaks, the otherwise cloudless sky more violet then blue. But violet is blue-amethyst, lavender and purple's bluish red as well. And all the greens mysteriously blue – the emerald, the hunter, the aquamarine. And the woods of the mountains, forever green, forever blue. Blue-mountain windrows trailing ridge on ridge, the subtle vocabulary of intermediate hue, blue on blue, a hundred shades of blue. And perennial blue I'll be, if I don't climb off this gelid mountain.

Another delightful day and average walk, I've logged eleven miles and climbed up and down four-thousand vertical feet as I reach the truck. The equivalent of marching from Mexico to Canada and back with a big close. Rustling in the bush an army of coatimundi pause from their foraging. I count a quick thirty-five, perhaps forty or more. Though frequently seen, rarely in troops this large. Then comes the big explosion and the long, striped tails fly in all directions.

I chase the westering sun across the wide San Rafael. A dirt road parallels the international border and charts its way across perfect prairie. The Mountains of Mexico articulations all blue and ambitious swells of golden grass hills cuddle at their faraway feet like spacious shifting dunes of sand. More grass, as I turn north for the Canelo Hills and home. I feel a song coming on…

> Left my dreams in Patagonia
> A sweeter love they'll never be
> I've gone down to Mexico… she waits there for me
> In Patagonia… Patagonia… Patagonia.

The last of the sun's rays flash across the silhouetted blue steeple of the Santa Rita Mountains. Across a broad table of grass, pronghorn are watching. The land is sinking under the weight of evening's blue shadow. The night here is like the day. All is blue and beauty.

> *"We lie in the lap of an immense intelligence,*
> *which makes us organs of its activity and receivers of its truth."*
>
> – Ralph Waldo Emerson

San Raphael

Chapter 17:
Hurry On the Day

Hurry on the day… hurry on the day
I might kill the old man and sing like an angel
Hurry on the day… hurry on the day
Faith bends my will His way… hurry on that day

Hurry on the day… hurry on the day
I would man-up to love well… as well I should
Hurry on the day… hurry on the day
In truth… in good… with wisdom would
Hurry on a work that measures me a man

Some distant day from here
When love and faith and hope adhere
"In quietness and in trust shall be your strength"
Now… that will be the day
Lord quicken contrite hearts as kettle-drums
On pilgrim paths till Kingdom comes

Hurry on the day… hurry on the day
I might kill the old man and sing like an angel
Hurry on the day… hurry on the day
Faith bends my will His way… hurry on that day
Hurry on the dreams that strand me here

Hurry on the day… hurry on the day
Now… hurry on.

Mount Wrightson - Santa Ritas

Chapter 18:
Exaltation in Temporal Canyon

"There, in the lucky dark
Stealing in secrecy... by none espied
Nothing for eyes to mark
No other light... no guide
But in my heart: that fire would not subside
That led me on... that dazzle truer than high noon is true
To where there waited one, I knew... how well I knew!
In a place where no one was in view."

– John of the Cross

Dilapidated in spirit after my crushing defeat in Nashville. And with the anguish and grief born with my realization that there is no salve or cure for the open festering wounds of my thwarted song writing aspirations, Patagonia has, if nothing else, been a soothing visual consolation for this wandering minstrel.

Sandwiched between the towering blue pyramid that is the Santa Ritas and the consecutive oak ridges that form the Patagonia Mountains nestles a quaint, tranquil community. Altered by a perennial stream from whose shores spring voluptuous stands of cottonwood, housing exotic bird populations from all over the southwest and Mexico. It is a place without debate, one of the fairest in first-rate Arizona. A pastoral paradise of endless, stretching prairie, forested mountains that birth rivers which sing across serene and untroubled valleys where pronghorn antelope wander still.

Temporal Canyon is a great trench that slides off the back of the precipitous slopes of the 9,400-foot Santa Rita Mountains forming a dramatic backdrop for our daily affairs. Since my relocation, I have walked the gorge countless times, for there is much to see and enjoy.

An intermittent stream courses through the canyon seamed with cottonwood, walnut and sycamore. Fish frolic, intelligible waters. Along the hills and hollows that form the grassy contours of the valley, oak-wood gatherings garnish the patent spaces with splotches of green. Deer sport through unfurling woodlands, bear hide in the conifer trees higher still and the lion, king of these wild dominions, roams free, though unseen.

I've climbed Mount Wrightson, the high peak many times, it practically being in my own back yard. Once again, I throw on the pack and head up the trail on a three-day mission. This is all familiar territory, one of my favorite places. I won't go into detail here of the mountains' great beauty, the outstanding forests, the symmetry of its skylines, this embroidered and uncommon landscape of wood and prairie. Suffice it to say, a land majestic and grand, which brings me to the reason for my scribbling. It is not what happened on the way up, but what happened on the way down that was really quite extraordinary.

The third morning found me camped at the crest of the range. After breakfast and a short stroll, I broke camp and headed down Gardener Trail for home. Snow lingered in small patches throughout the cool conifer forest. Steep descending paths presented wondrous views of the mountains' crescendo, a towering stone citadel, as stirring lines of canyon and ridge plummeted to meet the graceful distant prairie far below.

It is with a ginger step one walks at times like these. The benediction of the wilderness, the freedom of these moments, the exhilaration of being there, I drift downward the trail fueled by the customary wonder of it all.

Onward the miles and the morning slide by. Dropping two-thousand feet to reach Walker Canyon Trail. I move along the crest and crown of a pine-packed, juniper-choked basin. Obvious bear sign in these woods and a handsome stream that flowed along one of the seams in a mountain wall, where, in the guarding Gamble oak, it was clear they would congregate.

Advancing, the miles unfold and so the late morning and now early afternoon. Finally reaching the head of Temporal Gulch. From a ridge, peering through pygmy forests of Emory oak, my eyes wander down the great furrow as it slides off the mountain. My truck waits for me somewhere at the end of this raveling ravine some six miles distant.

I have been walking for hours. The rhythm of the trail, the

cadence of my marching feet, my labored breathing, my pounding heart, the weight of my pack, the hot dry air, the beating sun, the pulsating breeze; I am moving with the musical flow of the day. There is feathery lightness to my step, a frivolity and buoyancy to my spirit. Though my feet are firmly attached to the earth, I am floating, just above the ground, a cork bumpily bobbing along the surface of a stream.

Although physically tired, I'm not totally spent; but the hum of my body engine over the miles has placed me in an almost trance-like, hypnotic reverie. Though this is not an apt description of what I am experiencing, it is with some anticipation that I expect my spirit to leave my body and my flesh to melt into the surrounding terrain.

Something bizarre betides me. An indeterminate something I could not begin or hope to articulate. Something quite out of the ordinary onset to transpire – something fanciful and transcendental. With no way to describe it except in stale clichés.

Always in walks like these, there is the exuberant joy, the sadistic pleasure in the pain of the physical march. This intoxication would be described as a runner's high but something far more and better than this, is happening.

My body is like liquid, flowing gently, smoothly gliding. With a congenial wizardly whisk and whirl, I am one with the universe, part and parcel, one and the same. The universe; am I. Waves of rapturous elation are rolling over me. A quiet, still, inner frenzy of great excitement and expectation is welling up inside me. I have stepped through some spiritual-portal, crossed quite by accident into the twilight zone.

Though nothing is out of place, as I am acquainted with each stone and plant and wild thing in this valley, nothing is the same. Turned inside out. It's a contradiction in terms, but I don't even recognize this familiar place.

There is a certain vision one conjures of Heaven and what its spiritual spheres might be like; the quickness of it all, the clarity of mind, the camaraderie of all God's creation, the unspeakable love and peace, the wondrous glory of it all, the unending edge-of-your-seat excitement that never dissipates.

What no eye has seen or mind of man conceived.

I have somehow been led to the Gates of the City. Everything looks like it's been shot through a gauze camera filter. I perceive as through a mist, this liberal land. It is perhaps, that I am discerning the spiritual atmospheres of the natural things placed before me. There's a conspicuous effervescence to every rock and tree, a celestial animation, an ethereal air. I drift through a dream more real than sleep provides. I am more awake and alert than I've ever been. I cannot get past this novel conundrum, that although I know where I am; for I know this place well, I don't recognize it.

There is a Quaker-calm about my person that is exquisite. I notice, of course, the sounds and the music that the day is making but note more wonderfully, the silent space between each sound. My throbbing heart is a pad of melting butter. My body is weightless. I am almost outside it. There is an undeniable sense and a certainty that something is going to happen, to take place, a visitation, an encounter; annunciation.

I hear no angels chorusing, though fully expect them and strain to catch the notes. Cognizant that I am not alone, I keep looking over my shoulder to see whose walking with me – not a peep, there's no one there. My heart is close to bursting with this confident giddy expectation that something is going to break and to befall. It is undeniable: as I seek to discern it, fumble to feel it, almost tangibly touch it; something is coming. At any moment the Heavens could open. If the Lord speaketh audibly to mortal men, my time is near and now.

Setting down my pack, for one of my many rests along the way, I speak to God in a conversational whisper. For anything louder than these intonations would shatter this blanket of silence and reveal me a screaming madman. "Father," I ask, "What is it?… What is it Lord?" Fully expecting a thunderous reply or a quiet cue to match my own, there is nothing but a peaceful church-like stillness.

My spirit, through this whole march out of Temporal Gulch is poised and fully prepared, with slender summons, to spring from my body. My triumphant jubilant heart impelled and quickened by the bias-beauty set before me and something insatiably palpable, that I can't quite put my finger on, has brought me to the edge of tears. I'm on the verge of a good cry, but the source of my weeping is a gladness and a joy. A mystical, inexplicable spiritual journey well beyond words. Quite real and wonderful; though not readily defined.

And so, I keep walking, and I keep looking over my shoulder.

In one more location that will be catalogued forever into my memory, I sit by crystal water pools teeming with fish. Tall verdant grass pads the margins of a restful stream. Walnut trees canopied its flowing course and the sun surges through the branches and rains on the liquid mirror like a meteor shower. A riotous calm, an exalted tranquility, a whist serenity flows within and without and all this, attended by an uncanny presence.

Unaccompanied in the wilderness for three days but since mid-morning, I have not been walking alone. In bliss, ineffable, there is someone standing just beyond the scope of my peripheral vision, that when I turn to see, I can't quite glimpse... but there is someone there.

"Lord Jesus," I confide in whispery penitent supplication, "Speak with me Lord... for I am listening... What is it Lord?... What is it Father?" But the sanctuary remains silent. I am not losing my mind and I am completely convinced I am not talking to myself.

And so I keep walking, and I keep looking over my shoulder. At about 5:00 P.M., I reach the truck, somewhat reluctantly. Since early morning, I have dropped five-thousand vertical feet and marched – some twelve-to-fourteen miles, not an impossible accomplishment in and of itself. But the last six miles of the journey was through some spiritual kaleidoscopic tunnel. A place out of space and not in time, another dimension, another realm, an inscrutable world tangible and real, though not corporeal or elemental, as is germane to this one. Look... there's the sign post up ahead!

"Now faith is the assurance of things hoped for,
the conviction of things not seen. By faith we understand,
that the world was created by the word of God,
so that what is seen was made out of things which do not appear.
For whoever would draw near to God must
believe that He exists and that He rewards those who seek Him."

– Hebrews 11: 1-6

I'm disappointed that the Lord has not spoken in some audible
fashion. Yet my faith is not the slightest bit shaken. And so,
with perfect conviction, being fully persuaded that He just
might… I linger by the truck a few extra moments, hoping
He'll change His mind.

"The farther you go into the desert, the closer you come to God."

– Arabic Proverb

Chapter 19:
I Got a Girl in Mind

I got a girl in mind… down south Sonoita way
Where green prairies roll perfect
And hold blue mountains at bay
I got a girl in mind… she waits for me this day
On a bend in Temporal Canyon 'neath Sierra Madré
And on that farm… there in her arms
I'll melt… like winter-snow past our doors
That fell on high slopes of emerald forests of oak
And raced to bless this valley below
I got a girl… I got a girl in mind

Yes, I feel sorry for those
Trapped there in the cities, with the lives they chose
They could be happy I guess… but that's not happiness

I got a girl in mind… and at the close of the day
On the road I'm wired and weary with emotions all frayed
I close my eyes to see… that star-filled canopy
That canyon and our cabin… on the porch swing we'd be
And with the dawn… with the rain showers on
Clouds blazing like the Fourth of July
That's how love can be… as she makes love to me
I haven't wings but no-doubt I can fly
I got a girl… I got a girl in mind.

••

Kate looks at me and you know that we're gone,
To a field where there's no one around,
And I get my guitar and I sing her a song,
We fall back to love on the ground,
And I'm home.

Red Mountain

Chapter 20:
Red Mountain Bear

*"There may be more to learn by climbing the same mountain
a hundred times than by climbing a hundred different mountains."*
— Richard Nelson/ *The Island Within*

Southern Arizona borderlands are stagnate and stilled with
June pouring on the heat. The mercury climbs past the century
mark. Santa Cruz County winces under the weight of a
summer sun. Just one more day in an endless string of sunny
days, hot and dry. The range and woodlands are a tinderbox
waiting for summer monsoons. Without any real precipitation
in the last six months, it seems all of nature should dry up and
blow away before that blessed day arrives.

I'm bored. I'll climb atop Red Mountain for the sixth time, up
to the fire lookout, for lack of something better to do.

Red Mountain is an appropriately named six-thousand-foot
peak. It is the first in a series of wooded ridges dressed in oak
and piñon pine that slide in a southeasterly direction from the
town of Patagonia, crossing the line into Sonora Mexico. It's
the home of the mountain lion, bobcat, kit fox and coatimundi,
of deer and bear, an occasional jaguar, but you can count yourself lucky should you catch a glimpse of anything that moves
through its thick brushy jungles. (I'm excluding here, the
wonderful bird life wafting up and in from the Sierra Madre.)

It is with reluctance that I walk in these mountains, though not
for want of ocular beauties, it seems that there's nothing
moving in them. They are not very high, barely pine-topped,
though tightly knitted, with not so much as a secreted source
for aspiring springs and no standing water encountered.
Tangled-webs deceive.

Halfway up the stifling heel of an escalating ravine, I take a
rest. I have been struggling through unforgiving thickets of
bone-dry miniaturized oak trees, whose half-clothed branches

reach up through the air like arthritic hands praying for rain. What little soil there is exists as powder. The marbly-loose stones under my feet have caused me to fall repeatedly like a drunken sailor in for his first tattoo. With the high temperatures, sweat pours off my brow stinging the eye. My shirt is ringing wet. Climbing a two-thousand-foot slope in this unkind heat is taxing.

Ten turkey vultures are circling just above my head, floating on the wind as it races up the whetted ridge. I can hear the air, as it works through their matted, mummy-brown feathers. They're scouring canyon walls for a meal and with that many eyes in the sky they haven't missed a thing. Though from my vantage point, it's easy to miss things that are placed right in front of me, but today I get lucky.

As I stand up, I look down the opposite side of the gulch. An oversized bear the color of cinnamon, a perfect match against the rust rock walls, is strolling casually down the canyon just below my position. For just an instant, between tree clumps, clots and clusters, I catch a glimpse. The bundled-brush is so thick I lose him in a wink and he will not be visually won again.

Had I not stood up at that moment, he would have traversed the canyon, his presence undetected. The way this cleft is cut, its walls closing in toward the upper peaks of the mountain and the direction the bear was traveling, he would have seen me coming. I have been stumbling and crashing through crisp brittle branches making a heck of a racket. Yet he strolled casually down a slope just across from me, quite close, silently stepping across the crunchy ground. I never saw him until he was past and below me. If there were twenty bears in this immediate area they would work through these thickets unseen.

I envision bear habitat as lush green conifer forest with timberland-floors bedecked in fern and flower, with tumbling clear streams to gladden the day. Bountiful meals distributed through the firs for wild creatures to gorge themselves.

The Patagonia Mountains are not like this. Though it is a landscape as near architectural perfection and grace as earthly eyes might hope to see, you could wander many a mile over its wooded corduroy and intermittent prairie and not find a drop to drink. And it appears there are very few eats available, at least this time of year. It is beyond me that a buxom, burly bear could live in these kiln-dry forests in temperatures exceeding one-hundred degrees and survive.

I climb to the top of the mountain and talk to the Ranger searching for fires across the rippling blue horizon. Then, for me, it's a long way down and back. I drink all my water and return to the ranch with a thirst unquenchable. The day's heat has sapped all my strength. Tall fizzing ice-filled glasses, of "The Real Thing," slowly bring me back to a vision of my former self and I think of bears without such luxuries.

Arizona wildlife is abundant, but elusive. The signs are everywhere, but try and catch a critter crawling. When you're lucky enough to stumble onto something big, it's a complete surprise. The bear was discovered three miles from our quiet Patagonian hamlet. Perhaps I should be looking just a little closer to home.

> *"God sleeps in minerals, awakens in plants,*
> *walks in animals, and thinks in man."*
>
> – Sanskrit apothegm / (c. fourth century B.C.)

Chapter 21:
It's as Simple as That

Give me the mornin' when the day is new
Give me that sunshine... let it pour on through
With a canyon to walk or a river rollin' fat
Well... I can be happy with that

It's as simple as that... I'm as simple as that
If you know me at all man... I'm as simple as that
It's as simple as that... I'm as simple as that
With that I'd be happy and you can count on that

Or better yet evenin' when the day draws to a close
With the clash of storm and desert... insert creosote in nose
With distant blue-mountains to watch
For inspiration you see
Well... I can be happy quite easily

No doubt I'm crazy... no doubt... but don't despair
This world is falling apart and I don't care
Bound and determined it will go its own way
Straight ahead in a circular motion

Well... I'll take the mornin' when the day is new
Give me that sunshine... let it pour on through
With a porch and guitar... with jazz rhythms to scat
Well... I can be happy with that

It's as simple as that... I'm as simple as that
If you know me at all man... I'm as simple as that
It's as simple as that... I'm as simple as that
With that I'd be happy and you can count on that
It's as simple as that.

Chapter 22:
The Fire Fight

"The longest way round is the shortest way home."

– Proverb

After months of wondering if the Santa Cruz County Wildland Fire Fighting Crew, of which I counted among it ranks, would ever see fire fighting action – time and patience rewarded me with at least enough to hold my creditors at bay. It propitiously placed much needed food on the table. For, sadly, apart from Patagonia's aesthetic privileges and the freedom to do my walking and song writing, short of this rural world catching on fire, how is a plebeian to earn an honest living?

The first skirmish took place on the Mexican border thirty miles southeast of our hushed hamlet of Patagonia. The golden corrugated oak hills of the upper Santa Cruz River Valley, sparked by a dry thunderstorm, burned for three days. A small fire, only four-hundred acres, it gave us our first test of online fire fighting – the intense heat of a marching wall of flame, the back-breaking work of fire-line construction. Until you have tried to cut down several Emory oaks with an ax – in temperatures, exceeding one-hundred degrees – you clearly don't know what real work is! Be sure to add the burden of bladder-bags, a rubber water bag strapped to the fire fighter's back that sprays a spittle to help suppress hot spots during mop-up operations. Include the fun of working through the inky nights with our helmeted headlamps spotting scurrying mice, rabbits and other nocturnal creatures, now with nowhere to hide, their lush grassy world reduced to black powder ash.

A much larger fire across the border burned for two weeks charring six-thousand acres. Mexico has not the resources to extinguish their fires; they just let them burn. This is not as bad as it sounds. Since fire is a natural course of events in the ecology of healthy forests, what at first appears complete destruction can be a blessing. Forests need fire just as they need the rain. A good balance between the two makes for happy western woodlands. Too much of one without the other can create a catastrophe.

From our side of the fence, under the flash of a full moon, armies of firemen ate steak dinners shipped in from local Nogales restaurants and watched the Mexican mesas define their contours in fierce flame.

The following day, our fire contained, we went home. There was nothing further we could do for Mexico but hope the winds would not bring us their predicament.

The season's big blaze burned the Swisshelm Mountains in southeastern Arizona. We were the first crew sent to the fire, that at the time, was just 150 acres. Because of the mountains' steep terrain and the unrelenting winds, the fire grew, as well as the armies of men sent to fight it, until the whole range was consumed – a total of nine-thousand acres.

For eight days the war raged. Our side was armed with helicopters and air-tankers dropping slurry, hundreds of men conducting controlled burns, bulldozers cutting fire lines, thousands of picks and shovels and axes hacking through the forest. The fire did whatever the hell it wanted, as all fires do, until the monsoon rains came – and that was that.

We slept soundly on dewy baseball fields at the local high school in the small town of Elfrida, close to the burning mountains, ate well in the restaurants docked along the calmed streets, spent our pre-dawns and days and into the late nights, climbing the Swisshelm canyons, scaling the steep slopes, conquering the mountaintops dressed in flame. Deer, javelina and mountain lions fled. I saw strong men melt before the flames, collapsing from the heat and physical exertion, carried away like dead men from battle. We worked with thirsts unquenchable. Fortunately, the State of Arizona supplied all the Gatorade we could drink. From huge iced coolers, vast quantities of the magic liquid disappeared.

The Swisshelms being quite close to one of Arizona's great mountain ranges, the Chiricahuas, we were provided exquisite views of the surrounding topography. As we endeavored to extinguish the flames, my eyes gazed across vacant valleys of chrome-blond grass to the sovereign heights of amethystine peaks. The bright sky clouds of evening were saturated with transcendent shades of claret, apricot and indigo hues, as the sun's rays worked the cumulus cloud columns, leaving even the aesthetically challenged, stunned and beguiled.

Thinking myself derelict in duty not to bring such edifying beauty to the attention of my fellow brothers-in-arms, I did my best to open their eyes to the art of it. But much to my surprise, they did not seem to notice, or could not see, or were too tired to care.

The big battle went down the fourth evening at sunset. After a reasonably quiet day on mop-up duty on the northern end of the range where our team worked to protect some ranch buildings and a small ghost town, a great wind came up. Miles away, on yesterday's section of the mountain, we had success-fully conducted intensely-controlled burns, preventing a fire that was boldly moving down mountain slopes and into the valley – a small battle won. But today's big blow let the fire jump our line; a massive fire cantered across mesquite and oak-filled plains.

Quickly dispatched, we joined the ranks of a great army of hard-hatted yellow-shirted firefighters, working to prevent the now out-of-control inferno from advancing.

Wildfires roar like passing trains. It's best to stand off to the side and watch them roll by, because they can't be stopped. Those in charge of the militias manning the battlefront are very careful not to put their soldiers in dangerous positions where lives can be lost. But in this one and exceptional instance, we were sent to a conflict that couldn't be won and where lives were put in real jeopardy.

The wind is moving at gale force. A wall of flame twenty-five-feet high scampers toward us as fast as a man can run. It is consuming everything in its path – the heat so intense it melts my safety eye goggles. The soup-thick smoky air brings our eyes a steady flow of irritant-induced tears.

Now the only way to stop this madness is to set a backfire, but the wind is against us – the flames so fleet, they will confidently overtake us. Our commanders, screaming orders, lead us into battle.

We attempt a quick fire line and try a futile control burn, but things are quickly out of hand. It goes down like a real war. Through the smoke and the roar of the approaching flame, with the fevered pitch of a losing battle, our lives on the line, like crazy men – we frantically work, but it is quite pointless. The fire is running us down – fast! It is stand and die or retreat and live.

The order is given to fall back. Two-hundred men scramble down through a rock-filled wash, a natural break for the flames. On the other side, we form an orderly line and in unison the brigade runs as fast as legs could carry down a cattle trail to a distant road, another natural break for the flames, and we let the fire have its way.

With the onset of darkness, the winds died down and so the fire slowed, but not before it burned itself right down to the very road we had run to for safety. At midnight, we threw in the towel after a nineteen-hour day.

For a couple of hours there, it was full bore excitement. I still feel the furnace heat, the reek of smoke and the sting in the eye, and hearken to the lingering haunt of thunder in the galloping flames and the whistling winds that drove it. I see fire fighters drifting in and out through the smoke clouds like specters and hear their muffled cries through the din of battle. I still feel the "after the tempest" camaraderie, fellowship and sympathies shared by those who have safely weathered a storm.

Wildland fires burn so rowdy and recklessly and can grow so large that nothing can be done. We fought for a few more days on the Swisshelms until the rains came and the incident drew to a close.

With eight major forest fires burning across Arizona at one time, we were assigned to a high-priority fire along the Colorado River valley – three-hundred miles across the state at the famed Bill William's River.

This historic river system flows across an impoverished landscape of little rain, where summer temperatures hover at 117 and almost nothing grows on the stone sterile landscape. But along the river it's a different story.

Thick jungles of tall reeds line the shallow waterway. Cottonwood and willow form an almost impenetrable fortress that protects a staggering array of wildlife. A rout of birds flying: ducks, herons and eagles. The river houses beaver, deer, desert bighorn and javelina. Lions sneak through the brambles and catch the unsuspecting. It's a natural wildlife refuge.

This is easy duty in a sensuous place. Almost eight-hundred acres burn, but it is mostly out by the time we arrive. Because it's such an important habitat, we hang around to prevent any potential flare-ups. We spend three days making sure.

Because the day's temps sizzle at 115, we work through the nights. It's cake duty – mostly sitting around and talking, sometimes sleeping. With the dawn, time to explore: pioneer grave sites beyond the riverbanks, beaver splashing in their ponds, bighorn sheep donning distant crags – a bizarre world where the bounty and green glory of the river flows through a land of lifeless stone.

After an eleven-day stretch on the Swisshelm and Bill William's fires, they sent us home. There were more fires in the weeks to come. One burned in the Mule Mountains near Douglas, another in the Tortolitas north of Tucson. Then the season wound down.

They worked us hard and the hours were long. After the Tortolita Fire was wrapped up, I found I had done a sleepless stretch of thirty-six hours. My body went into a total melt down. Reaching Patagonia at seven in the morning, I said, "I must lie down to catch a few winks," fully expecting to rise after a short catnap and accomplish something for the day. When I opened my eyes, it was pitch black. I had been unconscious for fourteen hours.

Those, not familiar with the state of Arizona, may envision the place as a waterless waste of endless sand and cactus. This fact is true enough. It is also a land wildly diverse and contrasts its dusty deserts with the largest ponderosa pine forest in the world, covering more acres than some countries claim territory. These woodlands are a priceless natural resource requiring wise use and stewardship. We learn as we go.

It bears repeating: Western woodlands need two things in almost equal portions- fire and rain. One without the other, over extended periods of time, can produce an ecological cataclysm of near biblical proportion. I fought my fires in 1989. But in the years to come, Arizona would experience historic catastrophic wildfires of unfathomable magnitude due to prolonged periods of drought and forest mismanagement.

What were once fires that burned 10- and 20,000 acres have now expanded to 100,000 at a pop. The Rodeo-Chediski Fire in the White Mountains in 2002 took 470,000 acres in one hellfire romp.

A natural fire regimen, for a normal healthy forest, includes a low-grade fire burning through the trees every twelve-to-fifteen years. This thins out the understory and keeps the forest floor open but the big trees left unhurt. The vitality of the forest remains intact. This is a good thing.

After many years of human suppression of wildland fires, our forests are thick with overgrowth. Now when they spark, they burn completely to the ground taking every living thing with it. This is not a good thing. We have to change our strategy.

I hate ecological issues because, as with theology, no one can agree on anything. People are so fixed in their differing heart-felt and intransigent positions regarding the environment that all you end up with is a fight. This explains why nothing ever gets done. We have only two options regarding our beloved forests: we can thin those trees or watch them burn. I lean toward the common sense of the former. Put up your dukes.

Wildland firefighting was darn hard, hot work and a lesson in futility. Forest fires burn big and do whatever they damn well please. Joining a force to wrangle with them is similar to doing a stint in the Armed Services. You are glad when it's over, but convinced that you have done something important. It gave me a much needed job. But it was, really, just one more excuse to be out on the land, to experience the weather and the vistas, the fun and laughter, the camaraderie, the physical exhaustion, the heat and thirst of it – wishing it would all end or hoping it never would. Drinking in the landscapes, seeing the wildlife, enjoying allayed conversations with fellow infantryman between the skirmishes and the frantic cries in the heat of battle – you experience the reward of teamwork and the feeling of being a part – and the helplessness of knowing forest fires, like nature herself, so big and unmanageable that armies of men are but a colony of ants trying to control the environment.

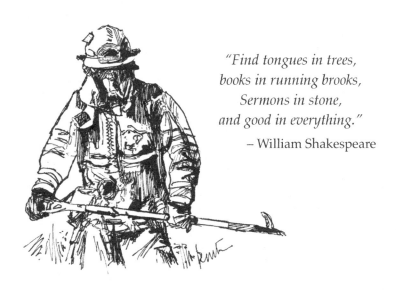

"Find tongues in trees,
books in running brooks,
Sermons in stone,
and good in everything."
– William Shakespeare

Chapter 23:
Ocotillo

An intense hot dry desert day
Un dia intenso caliente y seco en el desierto
In a typical Southwestern way
En la manera tipica del suroeste

Down by the river that just runs for a day
Alli por el rio que solo corre por un dia
I saw the mission heard guitars as they played
Vi la mision escuché las guitarras mientras tocaban

And it took me away, with the sounds of the horns
Y me llevó de allí, con el sonido de los cuernos
And the songs as they played
Y las canciones mientras tocaban

It seemed to call me right into the past
Parecía que me llamaba directo al pasado
I'm a Spaniard as long as it lasts
Soy español mientras dure

I wandered in just to hide from the sun
Entré como si tal cosa para esconderme del sol
Too hot to walk, could barely stand, wouldn't run
Demasiado calor para caminar, apenas me podía parar, no corría

I found some shade and I dropped to the sand
Encontré un poco de sombra y me caí en la arena
But cut my hand on Ocotillo… Ocotillo
Pero me corté la mano en Ocotillo… Ocotillo

High in the canyons where tall cactus grow
Muy arriba en los cañones, donde crece el cactus grande
Where the rain cuts rock but it cuts it slow
Donde la lluvia corta la piedra pero la corta muy lento

I wandered aimless to where God only knows
Caminaba sin rumbo hasta donde solo Dios sabe
Far from towns and ranches where nobody ever goes
Muy lejos de los pueblos y ranchos donde nadie nunca va

And all time stood still with creation flowing
Y todo el tiempo se paró con la creación fluyendo
In that silent stillness
En esa tranquilidad silenciosa

Birds broke the quiet as they flew to the sun
Los pájaros rompieron el silencio mientras volaban hacía el sol
And as the day turned to run
Y mientras el día empezó a correr
I saw some deer come and drink from a stream
Vi vengado llegar y beber de un arroyo

I pinched myself, I thought it might be a dream
Me pellizqué, pensé que a lo major era un sueño
They caught my eye and they darted away
Me llamaron la atención y desaparecieron

Past Ocotillo… Ocotilo… Ocotillo
Más allá de Ocotillo… Ocotillo… Ocotillo

Now that I'm back east my life's a mess
Ahora que estoy de nuevo en el este mi vida está en desorden
I dream of a girl with dark hair and long dress
Sueño con una chica con pelo oscuro y un vestido largo

She stands on a hillside where the ground stays dry
Ella se para en un cerro donde la tierra se queda seca
And look… she's standing by
Ocotillo… Ocotillo… Ocotillo
Y mira, está parada por
Ocotillo… Ocotillo… Ocotillo.

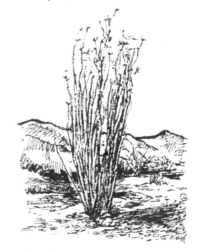

Cinder Fields, Pinacate Reserve,
Sonora Mexico

Father Kino

Chapter 24:
Sierra del Pinacate

"The Pinacate country was all about them,
outcroppings of jagged lava and the cholla. It was ugly country.
Far off he could see a bighorn watching from a volcanic cone.

The old gods lurked among the mountains
and the Pinacate was a place of the gods,
as all such solitary places are apt to be."

– Louis L'Amour / *Kid Rodelo*

There are deserts and then there are deserts. The Pinacate is a six-hundred square mile volcanic field in the northwestern corner of Sonora Mexico. If you landed on the moon, you might get some idea of the chancy, eccentric landscape that stretches south of the U.S. border to the Sea of Cortes. It is a wasteland of craters, cinder cones, shifting dunes of sand and molded-magma flows. A voluminous volcanic mountain sparsely decorated with Sonoran Desert plants and animals. An archeological storehouse relatively untouched by erosion or man.

For thousands of years, Indians have occupied the area. They centered their lives round natural water tanks called *tinajas*, lived unhoused on the open deserts, made trails from one water hole to the next and down to the Gulf. Their trails remain on the desert floor just as they left them.

I have read and heard so much about this place and for so many years have come to see what the Pinacate is all about and to find a trail and walk it. It is with a great deal of respect I come exploring this intimidating desert.

Here is a land that receives three-five inches of rain a year if it's lucky. Where summer temperatures hover at 118 degrees: moonscapes of rock and sand rival all beauty in waste-barrens. Insult to injury, this is Mexico, where even the good roads aren't. No adequate maps are available for the area. The only one I get, tells me to be prepared; the roads are bad. If something goes wrong, it says in big bold letters: **YOU'RE ON YOUR OWN**. Basal wreck roads, no water for your way, no people, no help if you get into trouble.

The recorded history there is fascinating. Just to the north runs *El Camino del Diablo*, the Devil's Highway. Melchior Diaz was the first European to face the burning sands in 1540, as indirect support for Coronado's Expedition. In 159 years, no white man dared try. Then comes the great missionary and explorer Father Kino, who seems to have walked every inch of the Southwest, making perilous crossings from Sonoyta to Yuma and back, as he endeavored to make sense of the lay the land and its possible link to California. This blistering waterless stretch of repellent desert is strangely seductive, notorious and deadly. With just a few *tinajas* in isolated ranges from here to there, for those who attempt a crossing, it's a roll of the dice. The Spanish Captain De Anza came next in the mid 1770s with a group of settlers bound for San Francisco. But the 49ers left the legacy.

If you want to read some sobering stories, read of those who did and didn't make it. This desert is as serious as it gets.

Geography creates its own destiny. The story there is the same as it's always been. A man cannot live without water. If you cannot find any, you will die. Hundreds did and still do. Today, these deserts are traversed both for legal and illegal reasons. For those who dare in the summer, this desert is prepared and continues to prove an undeniable fact: you will not walk long through its heat and live.

"Mile after mile, the gray sands stretched away
into the vague pre-dawn light, here and there,
a bit of white where lay the bleaching skeletons of horses
who had died on this road, known for so many years
as El Camino del Diablo, or the Devil's Highway.

During the few years when the road was followed
during the gold rush, more than four-hundred people had died of
thirst, and the vague line through the sand hills and ridges of naked
rock was marked by whitening bones and the occasional wrecks of
abandoned wagons. On his first trip over the road, he had counted
more than sixty graves in a day's travel, and nobody knew how many
had died whose bones lay scattered by coyotes and unburied."

– Louis L'Amour / *Last Stand at Papago Wells*

I am approaching two-hundred road-miles, southwest from Tucson. Mexican Route 2 trails still farther west across a land of sand and toothy mountain ranges. To the south I can see the familiar profile of the Pinacate and the massive lava flows that stretch across the plain like an ugly scab on a healing wound. Turning south, on the only path that gains me access into the area, a road that is basically running north to south, parallel to the range perhaps ten miles distant.

The desert floor consists of rolling fields of rusty black cinders, planted with organ pipe, saguaro, ironwood, silver-cholla and senita cactus. The road works its way along miles of lava flows. These fifteen-foot high rivers of once-molten molasses push out across the expanse like bulldozers, forming extensive heaved-up plateaus of crimped and crumpled rock. The intaglio I trek can't find a way up and over this titanic obstacle, so it works its way along its contours, as I hone in on *El Elegante Crater.*

There are nine giant craters, called *"maar"* volcanoes here in the Pinacate. Like impact craters on the moon, they are deep round pockmarks on a funereal landscape. My truck climbs half way up a flat-topped hill and I sense it's what I've come so far to see. Comporting up and over the rise, I stare into a bowl eight-hundred feet deep and a mile wide. Directly across the aperture yawning, a multifarious volcanic-shield forged and formed and the twin conical peaks of the Pinacate rising as bastions in maroon. To the north, red volcanic cinder cones from which brown rivers of lava flow from their bases, out across the black floor of an expanding valley to the east. Peewee elephant trees spring from the rocks at my feet, their thick trunks peeling a papery bark, procure an almost tropical look to this 'Star Trek' movie set.

In 1910, the Norwegian naturalist and explorer Carl Lumholtz wandered up the hill and peered into this sepulchral-hollow and dubbed it – *Elegante.* He had a way with words.

I make a loop around the swimming edge of the big black bowl and drop off its western shoulders to do some exploring. This inelegant landscape is completely unexpected, the shear economy of the place. It is a curt Kingdom stark and barren and in that lies the charm if there is any. A despondent baffling beauty stern and unearthly, dissident and bluesy, spiritually astringent, novel and compelling. I am a stranger in a very strange land and a kind of fearfulness undefined is a nag and a taunt. Less over this precarious and peculiar place however, and far more, over these rough and tumble roads and my truck's ability to navigate them.

A diligent search for words could not define this recoiling, surreal terrain. I'll try and find a few to describe how I feel on the inside and the welling up of a million confusing and conflicting emotions.

> *"It came over him all of a sudden that he had not grasped*
> *the stupendous nature of this desert setting.*
> *There was the measureless red slope, its lower ridges*
> *finally sinking into the white sand dunes toward the blue sea.*
> *The cold, sparkling light, the white sun, the deep azure of sky,*
> *the feeling of boundless expanse all around him.*
> *Southward the barren red simply merged into the distance.*
> *The fields of craters rose in high, dark wheels*
> *toward the dominating peaks.*
>
> *When Gale withdrew his gaze from the magnitude of these spaces*
> *and heights, the crater beneath him seemed dwarfed.*
>
> *Yet while he gazed, it spread and deepened and*
> *multiplied its ragged lines.*
> *No, he could not grasp the meaning*
> *of size or distance here.*
> *There was too much to stun the sight.*
> *But the mood in which nature created this*
> *convulsed world of lava seized hold upon him."*
>
> – Zane Grey / *Desert Gold*

I arrive in the Pinacate having logged many a mile on foot across feral Arizona and I have loved every aching moment. With every step, I am presented with the paradoxical attraction of wilderness. As an artist, I am compelled to move through it, to experience the weight of its beauty, to glory in this creation. Then, in coming back, trying to fashion something out of it.

Walking across wilderness has as much to do with meeting its physical demands and participating with the exterior landscape, as it does dealing with the interior one. In spectacular, empty, and sometimes dangerous lands, you are quick to perceive the bare essentials. I have a lot of experience in this department. I've learned a few lessons.

The secret to life is love and use. The fact that I have not been able to translate my love and this humble gift of song into a practical useful item, not just for myself, but for others as well, has left a hole in my heart so big, you could drive a truck through the chink. The catch is, it actually can't be done. But spending too long a turn in these resplendent outback's over time, becomes selfish and self-serving if this cannot be accomplished. Jesus was tempted in the wilderness, but he also came back and got some work done. I need to do the same.

For God is a perfect man and found among men. Apart from the rune charm that is the wilderness, there is nothing there but something altogether beautiful. If in the end you can't share it with someone, photograph it, write about it, or fashion a song, is it anything at all? As a man I too must dwell among men. Yet when I return to the city and see the mess men make with the streets and the traffic, the incessant building, the shroud of dirty air that hangs like a halo above its compounding confusion, I am left cold as a stone. I want to run back to the unkempt places. Only to discover again, I don't belong there.

Having logged so much time in these wild locales, have I grown weary of them? Has a maturity of years brought me beyond these things? Apart from loving these places with my whole heart, is there anything I can do about it? It melts down to the big questions. Who am I? Where am I going?

For the immediate future, its south, about twelve miles, to find a side road westward leading, that will take me to the base of the high peaks of the Pinacate. A rude cinder trail moves out across the disconsolate valley, turning into a caliche washboard road so rumpled and munched raw, I fear the vibrations will reduce my truck into a collection of unbolted steel parts. What worries me more, there are long runs of soft sand that scare me to death; I've been caught my share of times, ill-started, it's always alone, it isn't ever fun. My stomach is tied in a Gordian knot. I'm bound to have ulcers before this day is through. Will this truck make it? Will I escape with my life?

As a starving musician, I've never had the kind of money to afford a four-wheel drive vehicle; it is times like these I bemoan my financial status. This trusty pickup truck has taken me into some wild and wonderful hair-raising locations. It can and can't do several things. It will walk comfortably and confidently over bad roads of hard rock and minced-cinder, but this soft sand is a suicide mission. An accident waiting to happen. I can feel it coming. And as always on these excursions, I am by myself. Where's a friend when you need one? I would happily dance across these distrustful deserts with a backpack, but driving here leaves me fearful and faint-hearted.

After I pass sandblasted Sierra Suvuk, a mini-mountain all rock rouged red, by a mile or so, I start looking for a road escorting west. Finding one, I come across two Mexicans. Their run-down pickup stacked high with illegally-collected firewood. I don't speak Spanish, but they indicate by their waving and gesturing hands, that the road I'm looking for is back the way I came. Who am I to argue? But a handful of miles north and my meager map, tells me they're wrong. It's too late to do anything about it now with the sun sinking over the horizon. I find a side road, charting more cinder-solitude and mayhem, it's heading northwest closer in toward the Pinacate. I follow it for a few miles, but it's not the one I seek. Pulling off the trail I make camp. Tomorrow's another day.

With distant song dogs baying, a huge orange moon hovers over the eastern mountains cooling-colors. After dinner, under its diffused light, I stroll across the black cinder hills through the blue night like some goblin on the spook. It is deafeningly quiet, silent as a sepulcher, hushed and still, with a garnet hued Pinacate brooding in the distance. I find a trail in the eerie moonlight as I head south and wander for miles.

"The moon soared radiant and calm, the white stars shone serene.
The vault of heaven seemed illimitable and divine.

90

The desert surrounded him, silver-streaked, and black-mantled,
a chaos of rock and sand, silent, austere, ancient, always waiting."

– Zane Grey / *Desert Gold*

Some things never change. This evening could be a hundred
years into the future or three-thousand years into the past.
How many centuries of silent nights and fiery days have
passed since ancient feet have tread this trail? I press on
through its haggard and haunt, pushing the limits, probing
deep into the hermetic darkness through the moonlight's day.
I guess because it beckons, because it frightens me, because it's
bothersome and beautiful, because I can.

Once on a walk in the Growler Valley, a few miles to the north,
I spent a lovely day making a twenty-two mile saunter across
the desert. After dinner as I so often do on these excursions,
I walked away from my fireless bivouac to stroll through the
moonlit night. I hadn't wandered far, yet when I headed back
for camp, it could not be found. I was very close, but it could
not be located. I kept making loops, little ones and bigger
ones, traipsing back and forth in the general area. Not ever
being terribly far from my intended destination, it took a
diligent two-and-a-half hour search to find that damn tent.

That was the first and only time, I've ever been so completely
lost so close to home. Tonight I wander miles from the truck
and walk right back to it, as though getting lost is not only of
little concern, but a complete impossibility.

Breakfast under the blazing cirrus clouds of dawn. With a little
more investigative work across the crass cinder floors, I'm
ready to go. It is a unique and fragile land. Just under the
surface-clinker lies a fine light brown dust. As you walk across
its black "Grape-Nut" exterior crunch, you break through,
leaving your foot's impression with a gingery earthen-powder
showing. Every footprint, animal spoor or off-road tire track
leaves a near permanent scar upon the land which explains
why the prehistoric foot trails the Indians left, are so clearly
defined. I feel guilty walking around and making a mess.

Proceeding southward, past Mount Sierra Suvuk, I find a road
steering west. Though I can't be certain where I am in this
monotone clutter of creosote, judging by my scanty chart and

local topographic features, at least I'm headed in the right direction. The road if you can call it that, is bad. But I've made it; so far so good. I begin to think more confidently that this old truck of mine just might push right on through.

Unbeknownst to me, a fact later to be revealed, the route I need takes a sharp right, out of this wash that the road has been using to its advantage, climbs across a tormented lava field, proceeds onward to the still far-off Pinacate peaks. The car-width path, upon which I ride, is thickly lined with un-varying creosote and obscures the turn. I cruise right on by – a fatal mistake.

Just a little farther up the wash, my truck wheels sink deep into the sands. Up a dry creek without a shovel; or almost. My worst fears realized and my heart descends, abysmally deep as my submerged vehicle. Eyes glance over to the map that sits on the seat beside me and these big bold letters stare back: **YOU'RE ON YOUR OWN!** It is 8:30 A.M. as I climb out of the cab and assess the situation. Oh, God, please help me! I am in trouble! I am several days walk from the nearest town, completely alone and in over my head.

My prayers fly as my hands dig. Wheels spin, digging a deeper grave. I've got one of those funky, collapsible, military field-shovels, but in this situation, it's nearly worthless. You would have to see my predicament to fathom how impossibly trapped I am.

Held fast by this dry quicksand and buried beyond the differential I can't go forward or backward; chained to a sand prison. It's amazing. I keep my cool. No curse words fly. I keep working. The hours pass. I offer up penitence, supplication and prayer.

With time, using branches, rocks and brush and with a helpful piece of a small sheet of corrugated steel I find in the desert, the truck climbs forward, out of the wash and onto its bank. I'm still headed in the wrong direction, but I'm on slightly harder ground. Still far from getting back on the road from whence I came and far from a safe getaway. The fact that I've maneuvered the truck to this purview is really nothing short of a miracle. It's 11:30 A.M.

The next course of action is to build a road parallel to the wash, about twenty-five yards and drop back in on the dry run and the road at a point where I can safely proceed and thus, escape to freedom. This takes several more hours of clearing brush, bushes and chopping down small trees, rolling away big rocks, as well as trimming thick canopies of iron-wood branches from the dwarf-timber that cling to the wadis' bank and curtain overhead; 2:30 P.M.

Another pickup truck chances the wash. I flag them down to prevent the unwary from entering the same sand pit quagmire and certain entrapment.

A friendly American couple are more than willing to help me in my pickle of a plight. They have a full-fledged shovel. We go to work.

Can't turn the truck around, so I have to drive backwards over the road I have fashioned. Rick, a schoolteacher from the Four Corners area, works the shovel. Laurel, a Tucson teacher, sits in the rear of the pickup bed for additional weight and traction. I'm a truck drivin' man.

The wheels spin and we dig them out. They spin some more. We dig some more. With a spring and a jump, the tires catch and we're on our way. It's a bash and a bump, through a whirlwind of flying branches, crisp-shrubs and clouds of dust. The truck lunges toward deliverance. In an eternity of just a few excruciating moments, the vehicle ends its roller coaster ride and we drop in on the safety of the wash, advancing liberty and license. With the settling dust-devil fogs, it is clear my ordeal is over. Hallelujah! Rick slaps me on the back and says "Welcome to Mexico." It's 3:30 P.M.

There is complete and unqualified relief in emancipation and a perfect intimidation, an outright fear, of being caught again. I want to give up, throw in the towel, to leave this cursed place. I can't stop thanking Rick and Laurel for their heavenly help.

Rick finds the road off to the right that climbs across yet another irksome, infernally-forged lava field and forward, to the far-flung Pinacate. He's convinced it's the one for which we're looking. " If I'm not back in twenty minutes, come up after me," he says, "If not, goodbye and good luck."

I sit in the wash trying to decide if I'm coming or going. Rick and Laurel do not return. I have ventured a damn long way to see this apocalyptic place. Fearfully, I follow . . .

"There were hill and valleys a-many, of piled-up hell fire suddenly grown cold. The lava glowed and scowled at the heavens and dared us to come on."

– William T. Hornaday / *Campfires on Desert and Lava*

The road is terrible, at best a cow path across the moon's surface. The only thing that could convince me that I'm not truly on our orbiting neighbor is the hanging blue sky, the occasional cloud and conspicuous foot trails and tracery etched into desert pavements. Climbing high up the mountain contours I reach the end of the line, a place called Red Cone. A cleft in the mountain side forming an ocherous arena with its odd looking rubric rock walls planted with a curious combination of sub-tropic cacti. A perfect little park and staging area for an assault on the peaks that stand proudly above us.

Rick and Laurel are boiling some water for tea. They invite me over for a cup and a chat. We talk about this bizarre, befuddling landscape in which we find ourselves. The crude pottery shards they saw on the ground near the *"maar"* crater McDougal yesterday. Because it's inordinately late in the day to do any real walking, Rick and I make plans to climb the Pinacate in the morning.

With an hour before dark, I take a short stroll; studying the mountains' topography and contemplating the best route up its slopes. From here, it's about a four-mile walk and a 2500-foot climb up a crown that might loosely be described as an ice cream sundae, but in measureless incalculable ratios. Mississippian rivers of molded lava sagging off the peaks like coagulated chocolate syrup, but in magnitudes unimaginable. These cooled magma flows extend over many square miles creating a physical barrier to be reckoned. An obstacle course of jumbled, crimp-crumpled stone that must be climbed over, in, around and through. The soft ice cream part of this analogy, the peaks above lava, are belittling pregnant piles of heaped-up crushed-cinder, that will want to roll out from under our feet like ball bearings as we the scramble up the 40-degree slopes. It should be an interesting ascent. This is it. I've made it, thank God. It's going to happen.

Standing in the shadows of the Pinacate, the late sun is flooding the eastern deserts and the expanding valleys far below. Distant ranges are saw blades gleaming as I head back to camp for dinner. I watch a fattened full moon rise in strains of cadmium sulfide. I spin my prayer-wheels of praise and thanksgiving to the Good Lord for my timely escape from the desert sands. If Rick and Laurel had not come to my rescue, I would still be down there digging. I can't now, nor will I ever, get past my fear of being trapped again.

At 8:00 A.M., Rick and I are on our way. We climb out of the devil's red throne amphitheater, across the scorched earth of a heavily bombarded cinder field, and start wading up the Vulcanian lava-rivers; through the ruination of a city; a frozen, belched-black-basaltic glacial flow, all crack and crevice, canyon and crevasse.

The lava is as hard as iron and sharp as knives. Springing from the sterile stone grow exotic elephant trees. There are pockets in the once liquid lava, where fine light brown clay collects, as well as occasional moisture, on the fallen floors of sunken rooms. Inside, grow desert lavender, yellow flowering brittle-bush, blue solanum, and little barrel cactus with bright red needles that look like rubies set in the Byzantine brownie mix; all planned and planted as an esthetic Japanese rock garden or the look of the world when its dead and done.

Beyond and above the lava, we scale the cinder cants. Ocotillo, palo verde and dense stands of Teddybear cholla dress the increasingly steepening slopes. We huff and puff, rest and climb while scrambling up the almost perpendicular mountain; reaching the top of Carnegie Peak, the ranges second highest.

To our surprise, the mountains' topography is not as anticipated. We assumed that a saddle tied the two highest peaks together. The Pinacate, the one we've come to climb, is a separate cinder pyramid off in the distance, another entire mountain to conquer and our hearts sink with the realization. The view is spectacular. A million square-miles of uninhabited desert and the Sea of Cortes mirrors the sky.

95

We plunge down the slopes skiing with the lose cinders, almost a freefall, and reach its black-barren base in ten minutes flat. We cross a firebombed, harrowed hollowed-out valley and climb up the Pinacate ash heap, which is higher in elevation then Carnegie, but not as inordinate and arduous, seeming somehow easier to scale. At the top, we sign the registry. Lunch for two.

In 1698, the Jesuit priest, Eusebio Francisco Kino, climbed the Pinacate. The Spanish believed California to be an island. From this 3,904-foot mountaintop, he hoped to see if Baja California was attached to the continent. But you can't quite tell. From this position northwestward, to the point at which the peninsula meets the mainland, is here obscured by five-thousand square miles, laid-waste; the Gran Desierto del Altar, a wilderness of tan Sudanese sand dunes, the size of Connecticut. To the south, blue waters trail and across the salted-sea Baja floats on the horizon; everything else is desolation and desert. I think Kino, a god.

Our variant route back to camp is an attempt to avoid the extensive split-splintered lava flows, but this is impossible. The penchants we choose aren't as steep and the walk seems more leisurely. Less burdened, our conversation flows freely. In a land so set apart, I'm grateful for Rick's company. A little after three bells, we arrive back at camp.

To reward himself for a successful mountain climb, Rick wants to head south to Rocky Point for a seafood dinner. He continues to display greater courage than I. I'll settle for just getting off this depressant meridian and home safely. Down the "not-a-road," rugged, ragged road we go.

On Mexican Route 8, we wave goodbye. Rick and Laurel turn south for dinner and the sea. I turn north for the border and home, convinced I have seen and experienced enough desert landscape to last a lifetime.

An extended tarry in the wilderness might be likened unto a draftee's stay in the military. During your tour of duty, you can't wait to get out. Your reluctance to get with the program. The natural dislike to follow orders not your own, the lack of freedom. You long to escape its conformity and its physical demands. You would be more than reluctant to sign up again. Yet, with your honorable discharge, you look back on the regimental experience as one of life's most rewarding.

In my mind's eye, I see long sun shafts shot through the clouds that play on the sparkling peaks of a distant sierra. Rolling volcanic gray cinder hillsides planted with nothing but blossoming brittlebush. A black moon-crater named Elegante. Blue ocean waters lapping a hundred-mile stretch of creamy-tan sand dunes. Flowering sunken rock gardens on lavender lava flows. Soft, sandy-brown washes that swallow green pickup trucks whole.

These and a thousand other images will play in my mind in the weeks and years to come. These intimacies, indelibly etched on the impressionable mind, will remain forever like the prehistoric foot trails on the fragile desert pavement of the Pinacate.

> *"The significance of the desert and mountain*
> *is not who resides here, but what we ourselves*
> *have left behind in coming."*
>
> – David Douglas / *Wilderness Sojourn*

Chapter 25:
Roads

Roads … they're leading out somewhere
Roads… they're bound to take me there
Dreams… they're all that I can see
This minstrel's life… the life, He's given me
These songs… express my joy and pain
My hope… that He'd soon come again
Time . . . to tell what must be told
That sends me down these roads

Roads are callin' and so I have got to go
I can't say where or just what's in store
Entrust the everywhere spirit
Would that angels keep guard
It's that still, small voice I've been listening for
It's led me out this door and down these roads

Roads… they're callin' out my name
Roads… this pilgrim's sweet refrain
With joy… search out the farms and fields
Tell the truth the Lord revealed
Love… that's all that we can do
Our faith… enough to see us through
Hope… that springs like rivers flow
That sends me down these roads

Westward bound, there's a peace I've found,
On a road that's westward bound,
With the engine wound, you'll be glory bound,
On any road that's just west of town,
On a road that's westward bound.

Chapter 26:
Whispers a Song

I sing the songs that I've heard on high
Beyond tall timber where grand glaciers slide
Down granite peaks that carve a sky of blue
Where cumulus incandescent glow
Could cast aspersions on this life we know
Down in the valleys where the cities grow and breed despair
But up there, I'll find rest for the spirit and peace in kind
Alone with the Lord and the wind whispers a song

I sing the songs that I've heard far below
On windswept prairies where the pronghorn go
Dry dusty deserts where the creosote perfumes the air
I'm an artist drawn to this esthetic scene
To marvel at the canyons and its color scheme
Palettes of glory formed in rock and stream and tree
Come climb these hills and see
The world as finely crafted tapestry
Embroidered rivers on the loom worked by hands Divine

Listen and hear nature sing
Tall mountain turrets like church steeples ring
Call this believer there to wandering
Through splendid hues of stained glassed skies
Listen... the congregation sings
This host of mountain plant and wild thing
To choir songs of joy and winter's sting
Under the auspices of Heaven's care
Listen... for it leads me there
Be still... and listen... listen... listen

I sing the songs that I've heard on high
Beyond tall timber where grand glaciers slide
Down granite peaks that carve a sky of blue
For up there, I'll find rest for the spirit and peace in kind
Alone with the Lord and the wind whispers a song
Whispers a song.

The Shell Trail

Chapter 27:
The Shell Trail

*"None other than this long brown land lays such a hold
on the affections. The rainbow hills, the tender bluish mists,
the luminous radiance of spring, have the lotus charm. They trick
the sense of time, so that once inhabiting there you always mean to
go away without realizing that you have done it."*

– Mary Austin / *The Land of Little Rain*

I have been thinking and dreaming for some time. Having heard of a pilgrimage, Indians used to take, from the inland deserts of Arizona down to the Sea of Cortez. A kind of spiritual quest, a walk for shells, for salt and for knowledge. A trek of a hundred miles, over the worst of what the great Sonoran Desert has to offer, which believe me, isn't much but a weird and bewitching wasteland.

The ancient ones would walk with what water they could carry in fragile earthen pots and moving from one water hole to the next, eating what they could find along the way and with the knowledge of surreptitious *tinajas* in the mountain passes, journeying along prehistoric footpaths to the sea.

I want to do the same as they. To test myself as they did, to walk the mute trails this century has forgotten. To taste and feel, to catch a glimpse of what their world must have been like, though I can never know. I've come for a visit.

Sunday afternoon stretched bright and beautiful, as well as the road running west across the Tohono O'odham Indian Reservation 120 miles west of Tucson to the deceased-mining community of Ajo.

I have everything I'll need for the six-day mission except a map of where I'm going. I plan to wing it. With just the knowledge of the drive to Rocky Point on the Gulf of California, my ultimate destination, and having spent some time in the wilderness of the Pinacate in northern Sonora Mexico, I hope to sense my way to the sea.

I'm not totally clear on how to get there. If I fail, I'll crack this one up as an exploratory mission. If I make it, all the better. I want to walk across a desert that has no end and get the gist and sum soul of the place.

From the small town of Why, just ten miles south of Ajo, where I'll spend the night, I have a hundred, waterless miles of desert to reach my goal. I worry not of snakes or scorpions or even the distance but I'm scared to death of running out of water. I've squeezed four gallons into my backpack and will foolishly carry two additional gallons in hand. Still, I worry over water.

Upon reaching Why, I query a gas station to see if I might leave my truck there for a week while I journey forth. I get the okay and head up to Ajo and check into a motel. I'll get a good night's sleep and set out at dawn.

Dinner at the Palomino, a small Mexican restaurant; the last time I was here, there were guitar players and singers and they were just bad enough to be good. Tonight, I'm practically the only patron, just one other table. The roast-beef special is out of this world. I linger over apple pie and coffee.

The morning-mountains are jet black, sharp cut silhouettes against the brightening eastern sky as I head south for Why. I park my truck, slip into the desert, heading southwest across the Valley of the Ajo. My sights set for Growler Pass, a notch on the distant horizon.

The daybreak-air borders on cold and the water I carry in my hands is frigid. In minutes, my fingers are throbbing. I maneuver over a barbed wire fence. An immense desert swallows me whole. I disappear into the scoundrel creosote, as timbered shafts of sunlight charge across the serrated ridges of the mountains to fill the valley with an agate-yellow flush and glow.

This is going to be tough. I am not a beast of burden. The weight of water is going to prove my greatest physical test. But the day is new; I'm ready for just about anything and with determination, I push across the flats.

The cloudless sky a bright blue blanket. A curious calm hangs in the still air. Nothing is moving but me – no birds, no sounds but my breathing and marching feet. Off to my left, perhaps ten miles southeast, Montezuma's Head, a towering 3,600-foot rhyolite finger in the Ajo Mountains juts into the sky, gilt in gold and purple shadows.

The valley is an immense surprise, a swimming ocean of space, ringed by a distant mountainous horizon. On foot, progress against such proportion seems all but an impossible task. But as the early morning hours slide by, I notice that little by little, I'm beginning to make a dent in the endless stretch of tabular-sweep.

This place is a wasteland in every sense of the word. A pink caliche flooring and well-spaced creosote clusters and that's about it. Washes rush across the beleaguered hardpan producing green lines of palo verde and ironwood trees. There is not a blade of grass to be found.

Walk a little, rest a little, walk some more and rest again. I climb another barbed-wire fence, tear a section out of my pant leg and struggle on. Far too much water! I'm a nincompoop to carry this much as it will surely break me. Sometimes I lay prone, stretched flat on the ground resting ten minutes, then lunging forward for thirty, drinking as much water as I can, just to be rid of it.

Three steer are discovered in a sere wash thicket and they watch in disbelief as I cross an unfinished, rudimental world. There are not three clumps of grass in this whole valley.

The forenoon and afternoon is a non-sequitur and a telling pantomime. The Growler Pass nears. By 2:30 the foothills are reached. Saguaros and cholla spring from the slumberous ground-work that is a series of rolling hills that come down from the rocky crags of surrounding peaks. Into the trenches, up and over a small hill, descending into another wash, up and over a larger hill. The caliche-clay valley is replaced with a chaotic rock-strewn unearthly beauty. Fields of rubble are sown over the stony acres, as though the mountains had exploded and debris thrown everywhere and anywhere and where it landed, there it lay.

Reaching the crest of the pass, I climb a mountainside to gain some perspective on my accomplishment and see what obstacles might lie ahead. I've come a good distance, perhaps fourteen miles, though it appears from horizon to horizon. To traverse such a road-less ocean of space carrying this much water seems a task beyond endurance. Pleased with my progress.

The collective greenery of the creosote wastes over the leagues of open space between the mountain ranges produces an eerie optical effect, as though the mountains are thrusting themselves above green misty clouds or are floating in mid-air.

To the southwest, Growler Pass struggles across the mountain ramparts, a jumble of hills, arroyos and deep trenches. An obstacle-course for this over-burdened backpacker.

I've entered the 300,000-acre wilderness of Organ Pipe Cactus National Monument, and those cryptic plants cling to the bare stone faces of the hills as I struggle over the higgledy-piggledy landscape. The day is quickly drawing to a close, which is fine by me. After ascending and descending one more hill and exploring an abandoned mine shaft, I blunder upon the one crude thoroughfare in these here parts. Bates Well is just a mile or so down the rocky road. The only drinkable water for forty miles. That's on tomorrow's itinerary. As the sun sets, I organize a camp just off the way and work on a welcomed dinner.

The sun burned itself into distant valleys and the sky cooled its flaming colors of apricot and carmine to lavender and amethyst, then a sparkling ceiling of stars.

It is December, time for the Geminid Meteor shower. Lying in my sleeping bag, I watch shooting stars fling themselves across the black night sky. Not one or two, but a continual fireworks display till dawn. So close, with a good catcher's mitt I could have brought them down from the near by peaks to warm my morning coffee.

With the dawn, I pry myself out of the bag. Partake of oatmeal, sweet rolls and coffee and I finish my first gallon of water. Then start down the road for Bates Well.

In 1886, a rancher named Bates, sunk a well along side the Growler Wash and began ranching. He prospected in the nearby hills and Bates Well earned a spot on the map. Old timers traveling the Tucson and Yuma road, stopped for water and the news. The Papagos on their salt pilgrimages, as I am attempting, paused for a rest on their sojourn. By the 1900s, Bates Well was a vital crossroad on the Ajo-Sonoyta road, when nearby mines like the "Morning Star" and the "Alice" worked the local hills. In 1927, a man wanted for murder was shot to death by an Ajo Sheriff's assistant as he attempted his capture.

In the dawn's early light, I pass by this small spot of western history; three windmills, two trailers and one American flag. The road pushes across the rest of Growler Pass and for a mile or two, I use it to my advantage to rebuff the difficult terrain. Carrying this much water is proving a most burdensome task, nothing short of torture. I can barely hoist my pack off the ground after a stay, which is too bad, because if not for the weight, this would be a walk in the park.

With Growler Pass behind me, I leave the road and hem the great escarpment of the Growler Mountains. I gaze across a wide and sweeping valley of colossal proportion. Three groups of mountains frame the distant horizon, perhaps twelve-to-fifteen miles away. The Agua Dulce Mountains are far off to my left; I believe these to be what I call the Lukeville Mountains and the town of Lukeville at their base. (I am wrong.) To my right, and worlds away across the valley, the Granite Mountains and southwest, the smaller Antelope Hills. Assuming things are as they appear and believe them to be, this should work out as planned. (I am making a fundamental mistake on the positioning of these mountain ranges and will pay for it.)

The Growler Mountains are rugged rocky terraces, lifted up like tabletops and from their heightened mesas, debris pours off the fluted slopes as a flowing, pleated skirt of rock. Thirsting drainages gush off each groove on the mountain forming arroyos and washes that race out on to the distant sweep of the broadening valley. Ironwood trees and palo verde cling to the droughty rivulets and appealing pavements of volcanic stone are formed over the rolling hills between each dry water-course. I walk for miles along this great rock wall that is the Growlers, negotiating the washes, hills and thickets of dwarf trees. (I should be heading south by southwest, but I'm wasting all my strength and energy, heading almost directly west. Don't ask me why. Though I have a compass; I don't believe it.)

I negotiate a barbed-wire fence on a north south axis; I am leaving Monument lands and entering the Cabeza Prieta National Wildlife Refuge: 940,000 acres of rock, sand and cactus. No change here since Father Kino: the same sun, the same sandbox and the same indeterminate distances. Cresting one of the low hills, I look up just in time to see a desert bighorn do a quick step into some stunted trees walling a dry wash. A few more miles and I change direction.

I set a course for the Antelope Hills, the middle mountain range on the far horizon, heading south across the valley. Surely the road to Rocky Point runs beyond these ridges. When I find that roadstead, I'll know I'm on the right track.

Leaving the Growler foothills, the rocky ground surrenders to the flat creosote valley. Gone the trees and cactus to a wasteland of creosote, good for nothing but to be crossed and then forgotten.

The ubiquitous creosote bush does have its conjuration and charm however; it's a survivor. Some of the oldest living things on the planet have been discovered in the California Mojave Desert. Spotted by satellites in space, they are great living rings of creosote, estimated to be ten-thousand years old. These larger clumps and circles, though they don't look like much, toughing it out, suffer patiently the insistent sun. In Mexico, the whisked shrub creosote is accredited: The Governor.

"To me the greasewood is a symbol for health and
an example of cheerful existence under adverse circumstances.
Through, strictly speaking, nothing in nature is ugly,
the greasewood could not be called beautiful,
except, perhaps, when covered in the spring
with its small yellow, jolly flowers.
It may be compared to a person radiant with health and
good cheer, for which he is liked, though he may not be handsome.
Were I a poet, I should sing the praise of the modest
greasewood of sterling qualities."

– Carl Lumholtz / *New Trails in Mexico*

The afternoon is spent crossing this crisp creosote strewn with only one memorable thing to note apart from my increasing confusion as to where I am in the grand scheme of things.

Delving deep into the valley and much later on in the day, I encounter the Growler Wash once more. This water coarse that started, perhaps twelve miles back at Bates Well, has charged afar-off the outlying flat expanse and runs, arguably another thirty farther on, before disappearing in the vast and vacant sands of the San Christobal Vale. It is a serious parched river. I marvel to think a desert that receives five inches of rain a year could, in a desert downpour, send waters racing crest-fallen from the mountain passes, set free and flowing athwart this thirsty clay floor of a measureless valley, without it being directly drunk dry at its source. Yet as I stand and observe the riverbed, it is clear that water has coursed through its arthritic veins with the impression of water left in the tumbled sands.

Stately palo verde and ironwood forests, ancient of days, cling to the powder banks. In a world of nothing but creosote, an oasis of green mini-trees minus the water. Birds find a haven in protective branches and a lone hawk works the empty sky. On either side of this great dry limitless arroyo, there is nothing but a lackluster greasewood waste.

The balance of the afternoon stretches a yen, F-14s race back and forth across the horizons. The land is good for nothing but the skies are good for war games. There are spent shell casings here and there and I stumble on to two bullet-ridden, military aerial targets.

At sunset, I rejoice in the day's end just to emancipate myself from the weight of the pack and lie down. I know what a pardoned prisoner feels when the door swings open.

The escarpment of the Growler Mountains from this far-flung orbit in the valley is impressive. A towering blue wall, twenty-five miles in length and a lovely shade of lavender air hovers over its stony architecture. The valley floor glows fluorescent pink in these sunset moments as though the ground is electrified. Until the stars take over, the earth has an incandescent life of its own.

Another evening of winging stars across the heavens. These

fireballs have become common place, as from all directions they race pell-mell across the glittering star fields. What a show! And through the night, as big a quiet as I ever heard.

"It is in the great wildernesses,
on lofty heights and on desolate deserts,
that one feels the greatest of Nature's mysteries.
In the starlit heavens, mind outruns vision."

Ralph Pumpelly / *My Reminiscences*

At dawn, I savor breakfast and really begin wondering just where I might be. I climb a dead dwarfed mesquite in hopes of gaining some perspective. With the sun's first rays, I can see some kindles beyond the Antelope Hills, which are now quite close. I assume these firefly lights are farms and the road of which I search. Along the Agua Dulce Mountains there are also star-like illumines farther to the southeast, where I believe Lukeville should lie. I play it safe and head for a mark between the two.

No longer being able to abide the weight of water, I obtain some absolution by pouring a gallon on the ground before I leave camp. At least now, I can lift the ponderous pack off the ground. One learns from one's mistakes; I've wasted too much precious energy carrying too much weight, with still a long, long way to go.

The third day out is one of great physical fatigue, increasing confusion and disorientation. The day's course is a broad southeasterly arc across the predicates of the mountains that form the southern perimeters of this massive parenthetical. After many miles and the burden of my horrid haversack, the lights I had seen in the morning proved to be nothing at all. After many more miles, the town of Lukeville, that I was sure lay at the feet of the Agua Dulce Mountains, declared and disseminated nothing more than wishful thinking.

Shocked, I turn eastward and set my sites on the southern end of the Cipriano Hills that form the eastern portals of this elephantine unending Growler Valley. (The hillocks were christened after a local hombre named Cipriano Ortega, who made "little ones out of big ones" at the Victoria Silver Mines.) Surely, one of the National Monument roads runs close to these peaks. Perhaps Lukeville is beyond this gatepost. If I can climb that rock pile, Lukeville can't be far. I'm sure I'll see it from that vantage point.

The sun is making a dash for the horizon as I walk across the backbone of two colossal piles of chocolate-brown, volcanic boulders. I am king of the mountain and king of all I survey. But across this boundless realm of waste, this measureless dominion of space, I am the only living soul. There are no roads, lights, no towns, or any indication whatsoever, should human beings exist on the planet. If Lukeville endures at all, it is somewhere else and far away. I am not only dumbfounded by the view, but at a total loss, as to where I might be. Fortunately, I am not lost but I don't know where the hell I am. Having walked from dawn to dusk, I am exhausted, physically in pain, completely befuddled and confused.

But what a view! Words are not to be found that could describe the complete and total desolation of it all. Inadequate my vocabulary, my meager linguistic skill in attempting to frame this defunct land and its grim glory.

From a mountaintop tipped-high above the desert floor, I gaze across this iniquitous wilderness, odd and curious. I cannot believe my eyes. The great Growler Valley draws out sixty miles in length and perhaps twelve or more in width. An oceanic interval of creosote looks like the great Australian outback, minus the impertinent plants. As I perceive the distance I've come in the last three days, I want to faint dead away – a gargantuan trackless landscape.

The raw geologic charm of the mountains' rugged ramparts stand proudly protecting the bedeviled wastes at their feet. While flanking facets slump off the heightened escarpments and fan out on to the flushed-flat indefinite dimensions and duly decorated with saguaro, organ pipe and palo verde. A mighty wilderness, gnawed barren and bare, filled with nothing but space and impaired beauty.

I cannot accept as true, that I have come this far, suffered this much pain and miscarried my objective. I have come a long way to find that I have failed to hit the mark, big time. Very disappointed with myself, my only course and remedy is to return by way of Growler Pass, from whence I came.

I limp down the mountain to my backpack and do dinner in the twilight, jumping into my bag for the longed-for rest. To lie down is heaven itself. The ebony night reveals three shooting stars. The wind starts to blow for the first time in three days.

> *"Like dead scale, the superficialities, the falsities,*
> *the habits that had once meant all of life dropped off,*
> *useless things in this stern waste of rock and sand."*
>
> – Zane Gray / *Desert Gold*

It is far too windy to work my stove in the morning light. I forgo breakfast until I can find some kind of windbreak. I pack up and start walking. A cloudy sky is a welcomed change from the less imaginative blue that I've been witnessing the last few days and it brings out the desert colors vivid and brilliant.

Marching along the footings of volcanic ridges that form the eastern walls of this oversized Growler Valley, I head for Kino Peak and the Growler Wash, for somewhere over there, now way over there, Bates Well exists, a ranger station and a wretched road to civilization.

Apart from the fact that I am in physical pain, walking with a halt and a hobble and want this damn tedious trek to end. Apart from the fact that my attitude stinks, that I am disappointed with myself, there is nothing I can do about my mistakes. The day is steeped in a marvelous light and a splendid color is brushed across this outlandish landscape. My mind's eye, like a photographic plate, has captured forever every captivating and desolate scene.

Gale-force winds are whipping the creosote to and fro and the collective bowing olive branches over the peeled leagues produces a yellowish-green, tempest-tossed sea. The volcanic mountains, the color of fudge, like over done loaves of sourdough, collect in the corner of the valley as sunbeams prod and pry through the cloud-holes and reveal possible passes through the strange arrangements of stone.

The early morning hours blow by like the wind. At 10 o'clock, I reach a lovely wash that is snaking its way across the flats as it pours out of the desecrated, burnt basaltic hills close by.

An aged palo verde shelters me from the harsh reality of the deadened dubious creosote waste on either side of its insipid shores. In the soft sand, I relax and enjoy breakfast, watching birds flit through the thickets.

With breakfast concluded, I bolt across the last few miles of level creosote barrens before reaching the furrow-like foothills of the Bates Mountains. My rudimentary understanding of geology cannot begin to fathom how such stone sculpture could be fashioned. The odd turrets of rock on the mountain-crests' creased crowns or how the desert pavements were spread out at their feet, or the time it took to create such wanton wonders, is beyond my reckoning.

It is for sure; this was once a land of fire. From the depths of a fiery underworld, God knows how long this landscape was flowing molten stone. Whether by volcanoes, mountain-blocking faults or fissures and left to time and erosion, this is a trash-heap world of cooled ash and cinder. Crossing the petrified gardens and stony pyrotechnic precincts, I gawk at the anesthetized rock pavements and struggle across this moonscape rubble for most of the afternoon.

Given the chance to create a landscape with no holds barred, your imagination running wild, no creative mind could conceive a world this originally inventive: an inexhaustible beauty, an omnipresent loneliness, an inconsolable heartache.

"For the garden is the only place there is, but you will not
find it until you have looked for it everywhere
and found it nowhere that is not a desert."

– W. H. Auden / *For the Time Being*

Some of the pavements are crushed, gray gravel, with larger black volcanic blobs of pitted boulders pressed into its surface, polished bright and shining like shoes from the elements. The washes are just trenches of rounded, smaller boulders fit per-fectly together and great ironwood and palo verde that spring from stony beds. All this chaos, leaving quite an impression.

To my surprise, a great blue heron is discovered in a waterless wash, not a drop of water for a hundred miles.

The wind begins to die down, of which I am most thankful, as

I am quite tired of chasing my hat with every wind gust. Having traversed these low lurid foothills of the Bates Mountains, I make it to the Growler Wash. Kino Peak is the dominating topographic feature and I know that I'm closing in on Bates Well and none too soon.

I am hurting, and pushing my body to its physical limits. My left foot is totally gone, not being able to apply any pressure on it. I walk with an exaggerated hamper and hitch. The right lower leg, where it meets the foot, feels like a nail has been driven into the adjoining ligaments. My shoulders are fists full of knotted muscles, my lower back bruised by the weight of carried water. Despite the torture I tolerate and the inclination to lie down and die, I have no choice but to press on.

The Growler Wash is a major river course, though waterless, there are times it's hard to believe when water pours through this pass like the mighty Colorado. The high-water mark of debris clings to some desert-brooms well outside of the wide stream's bed. The torrents-careening have carved and gouged out great pockets in the sandy bottoms the size of dump-trucks, that after the initial rush of water, becoming holding tanks until the sand drinks it dry, leaving powder dry mud-cracked craters as I find them now.

Walking over the dune soft sand is like walking up a down escalator or swimming against the tide. I'm making progress but it's negligible. Jungles of thorny brush exist where the sand doesn't and it is equally hard to negotiate, but with the struggle, I'm putting some miles behind me.

Though distance in this desert world can be deceiving. Something that appears quite close, might be ten miles off, or something you could reach out and touch, could be a walk of two days. One can never be sure. I'm growing unsure once again.

Having walked now a good distance up the Growler Wash and judging my progress by Kino Peak, knowing the ranger station and Bates Well lay close to this landmark and in this wash somewhere; I must be all but home. So dropping my pack, I climb up a rocky-rime to an aerial view of my position. In the next few moments, my world came crashing down.

"Out of the abundance of the heart, the mouth speaks." I hope the Lord isn't listening, for more than a few imprecations have passed my lips this day. Out of shear frustration and fatigue, faith falters.

As far as the eye can see up the wash, there are no signs of life. No road, it can't be far. No windmills, they should be right here. Have I come all the way up this pass only to have missed that for which I've come? Like everything else in the last few days, nothing has been where it should be, or I thought it would be. Fortunately, I'm not lost, but I don't know where the hell I am. My exhaustion complete, my spirit broken. Profanity sootheth not the savage beast.

No option, but to keep walking. A mystery as to where I find the strength. A few more miles... just a few more miles! After an appropriate distance, I climb high another desiccated cant. And what to my wondering eyes should appear – an American flag! Praise God Almighty! I wonder, can I go the distance before dark? I do. Though not in short order, my dopey doddering is transporting me to the gates of a city: two trailers, three windmills, and one American flag. Since morning's first light, I have walked the day long. I am very tired. Very tired. Lie down dead tired.

As I enter, a frail, old couple, are huddled over a rusting oil drum and are busy bagging ashes. Setting down my backpack unnoticed, I walk over and say hello. They seem almost as surprised as I that others live and breathe, equally excited and relieved to be able to talk to someone other than our own selves.

Explaining my situation, my hope of getting a ride from someone wending this road less-traveled, back to Ajo, or any other place for that matter, and of my adventure of the last four days, they invite me in for some coffee.

It's like old home week. They are warm and friendly and I, the prodigal son. It is quickly decided that since tomorrow is their day off and they'll be going to Ajo anyway, I should ride along. I have not the strength to argue. It's settled. Inside a small trailer, around a tiny table, the coffee is sweet and the conversation, warm. The sun goes down as I listen to an endless string of great stories.

Roy and Fran Camper, a brother and sister team, are the

caretakers here at Bates Well, permanent residents of what remains of the historic ranch. If left unattended, the ranch house and windmills and stock-pens would be destroyed, so the government makes sure someone is always watching. Having worked in Joshua Tree National Monument for a number of years in a similar capacity, they were transferred down to Organ Pipe and have been enjoying their retirement just hanging around. They're filled with the stories I love to hear.

Like the time a jaguar came in for a drink at the water trough. They are practically extinct, at least north of the border, but one stopped in for a sip and then quickly retreated into the great outback that surrounds this two-person outpost. What Roy called, white Mexican fish wolfs, up from the gulf have done the same, as well as deer and bighorn sheep. I am too tired to talk but unexpectedly animated with these tall-tales.

"You must stay for dinner," Fran says, as she slips some chicken pot pies into the oven and Roy's stories unfold as a continual string of pearls. A retired Navy man has a lot to tell. We cover a lot of conversational territory; music, wilderness, California, Arizona, guns, smugglers, poachers, illegal aliens, weather, mining, the Park Service and on it goes. Dinner disappears but the stories don't and the evening trundles on, unhurried.

No television on the ranch, just a radio; Fran likes to listen to "Radio Play House." It's time for the show. John Wayne and Jimmy Stewart are starring in *"The Shootist"* and we're transported back to the 40s and totally entertained with John's singular swagger, the footsteps, the door slams, and Jimmy's distinctive stammer; all this, augmenting a quaint and curious evening. Later on, it's a detective story, as we wonder who done it. Then it's more coffee, and Roy rambles on till midnight. They tell me that they sleep late into the morning. I tell them I'll take a walk and see them, whenever. "Pleasant dreams," as I step out of the trailer and into my sleeping bag.

Close my eyes and when I open them it's morning. I am in no rush to get up; I am barely able. Around 10 A.M., I have some breakfast as a curious coyote scrutinizes from across the drive. I manage to stand (a near miracle). I grabble and grope, a short

114

walk along the Growler Wash and climb a mountainside.

From the heights, I look out across the Pass and beyond; so far the Growler Valley voids and arena of my struggle. I've got the blues about not accomplishing what I've set out to do, a little embarrassed to tell friends of my failure. I try and console myself with the thought that this defeat has been a learning experience. After all, it's easy to get lost when you don't know where you're going.

Downing slopes – nothing but boulders black-boulders and nothing more. I explore the ranch remains: a stockyard, adjacent windmill, water tank and bunkhouse. I am just too physically spent to do anything but sit down. I wander back to the trailer and sit by the water trough and watch birds come in for a drink. I try and write a few notes; even this requires too much effort.

Around 2:30 P.M., Roy and Fran are beginning to stir. Late sleepers for sure! After their breakfast they invite me in for some coffee and the stories begin again. One interesting note. In a small book in which they keep the daily temperature, wind and rain, I scan the records. Summer temperatures average 107, with hot days as high as 114. Less than three inches of rain for the year, yet many times, they have seen Growler Wash run like a raging river. The water, they use for coffee is pumped up by the windmill just thirty-five feet below the surface.

At 4 P.M. we jump into a pickup and head north on a derelict rough-and-tumble road twenty miles to Ajo. Stopping at the pharmacy to get some medicine for Fran's back and after shopping some groceries, they insist on dinner. Fran says, "It's a long ride back to Tucson."

A relaxing meal and more of Ray's anecdotal-meanders; they won't even let me cover the check. I hate to see this come to an end. They've become my surrogate parents. I know they were pleased to have a visitor come to call in their remote world. Back into the pickup for the short ride down to Why and my waiting truck.

It's many good-byes, a hug from Fran and a Merry Christmas wish. My exploits draw to a close.

In four days of walking, I've covered sixty miles and learned some lessons about the lay of the land and the weight of water. Apart from the excruciating pain in my left foot, that will take two weeks to ameliorate a healing, it's been a good experience.

In the years to come, I will make several more inquisitorial cross-country treks back into the Growler Valley and become better acquainted with this immense empty desert. In retrospect, can't believe I made the mistakes I did on this walk.

It is laughable to think you can walk very far carrying six gallons of water. I knew that going in. However, not being familiar enough with the lay of the land at the time or the proprietor of an appropriate vehicle that might transport me to a half way point where I could cache water and then walk to it; which is the only way this can be accomplished. I hoped that my physical prowess would be enough. It is not enough. I am not Superman, nor am I Charles Bowden.

The other blunder, was in being far less concerned about the first two valleys I had to cross than about the formidable wasteland of the Pinacate, the last half of the long journey. Misinterpreting the Agua Dulce Mountains for the Sierra's southeast of Lukeville on the Mexican side, led me too far to the west of my intended destination and many unnecessary miles eastward to discover I wasn't where I thought I was.

Often I have wondered how far I would have fared carrying just four gallons of liquid-life. Winter temperatures are mild and water requirements not as great. Even with my directional mistakes, the Pinacate lay just a hair beyond my view. Once that mountain was sighted, I would have known exactly where I was. Would I have had the strength at that point to continue? This is shear speculation and water over a waterless dam. I live with my mistakes.

However, after four days and sixty miles, I was incapable of going any farther. Even had I put these miles in the right direction, I would still have forty-plus miles to go and therein lies the rub.

It is clear those who made the pilgrim's journey did so with nothing more than resolution, a little carried water and very little else, while moving expeditiously from one *tinajas* to the next in a beeline to the sea. No dilly-dally here. Any additional burdens inflict penalty and prove a desert discipline: Come prepared or become me.

The Growler Wash has long been a corridor through which ancient man journeyed. A few miles east of Bates Well there are very clear petroglyphs carved on jet-black-boulders heaped-high above the arroyo. A kind of sign-post at a migratory crossroads.

As for the men who fashioned them, who lived and walked across these deadly deserts and down to the sea; modern man with all his convenience and technology, can't begin to comprehend their world. It could not have been a life of abundance. They were forced to be minimalists, this spare landscape would have seen to that. But they knew something that we don't. How to live within the perimeters of what the land could provide. The fact that they did it successfully for millennia is a testament to the endurance and tenacity of the human spirit and its commitment to job-one: Survival.

The western deserts of Arizona and northwestern Sonora Mexico are wonderfully unique, emaciated and austere, with an acerbic-charm all their own. Because they're so open and spacious, it's fun and quite easy, when it's not hot, when you're not carrying much water, to walk a great distance over this terrain in a day. So I keep coming back and I keep walking.

In conclusion: These deserts are very serious business. Only a fool travels there in the summer. Treat them with the respect they are due. They are places, scary big and empty. Many have lost their lives.

Proceed with caution.

> *"The land of lost rivers, with little to love;*
> *yet a land that once visited*
> *must be come back to inevitably."*
>
> – Mary Austin / *The Land of Little Rain*

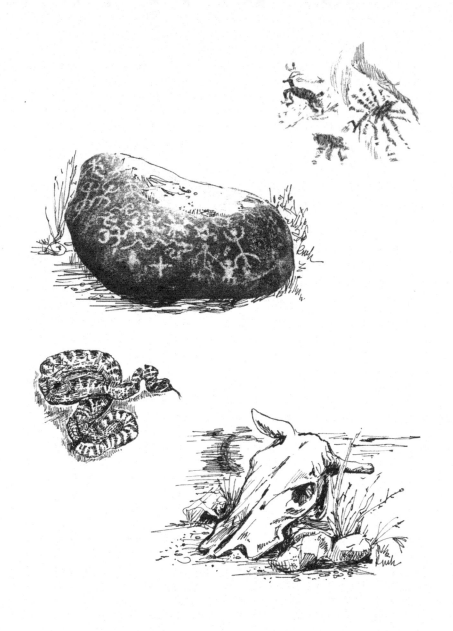

"After the making of Eden came a serpent,
and after the gorgeous furnishing
of the world, a human being."

— John C. Van Dyke

Chapter 28:
Going... Going... Gone

Before this city came sprawling
Before this desert was filled with streets and homes
Before the rivers stopped running
Before the traffic stood still
Before the Spanish in search of their cities of gold
Before the Anglo came stealing
Before the snowbird took wing in search of a home
Before the natives lost theirs
God made this beautiful place

But it's going... going... gone

Now I know that the Lord has made the world a field
Raising folks up to Heaven through the Son He revealed
But I can't help but worry as we plunder and sack
That this place won't be ruined by the time he gets back

Cause it's going... going

Gone the simple red man dreaming
Come the population teeming
Gone the open space and air
Complete with modern man's despair
Gone the hope we'll one day see
A land more glorious wild and free

Cause it's going... going... gone

Before this city came sprawling
Before this desert was filled with streets and homes
Before the rivers stopped running
Before the traffic stood still
Before the Spanish in search of their cities of gold
Before the Anglo came stealing
Before the snowbird took wing in search of a home
Before the natives lost theirs
God blessed this land and this place

But it's going... going... gone.

Buehman Creek

Chapter 29:
Buehman Creek

A desert represents "the absence of truth."
Natural water – "spiritual truth,"
and rivers — "truth in abundance."
"Come ye, yourselves apart into a desert place
and rest a while." Walk this desert and learn.

Buehman Creek is the only living stream on the eastern face of the Santa Catalina Mountains; that in and of itself makes it an extraordinary phenomenon. The only flowing water on a huge tract of empty desert filled with creosote and saguaros. What is also unbelievable, on the southern and northwestern faces of the Catalinas there are nearly a million people living. I have spent many years walking and taking photographs in this canyon, and Kate shares a sketch with you here.

A sketch is worth a thousand words. I keep coming back and shooting my favorite locations again and again. What is a constant source of amazement to me, in a place you might assume should remain reasonably static, the exact opposite is true. It is a land that is in a constant state of flux and metamorphosis. Not in a subtle way but dramatically, not every now and then, but on a near daily basis.

A major flood will move through the canyon erasing stream-side-thickets of cottonwood and willow. Rearranging the beaches and reefs of river rock. Seedlings will quickly establish themselves. In a handful of years, the prodigy stands twenty-feet tall growing swift as bamboo. A few more seasons left undisturbed, a full-fledged forest of fifty-foot trees. A timber-grove, near impenetrable. A big storm will stall over the Catalinas and a fifteen-foot wall of water will sweep through the canyon, vaporizing those forests, leaving a few esthetically, well-chosen trees and the process begins anew. In places where the stream was a babbling brook flowing over cobble-stone, the deluge has hastily excavated Olympic-sized pools of waist-deep water.

What at first, appears to be complete destruction is actually a blessing, just as fire is both destructive and beneficial to a forest. Floods do the same for desert streams. Not only enhancing the canyon visually, but creating better fish habitat, improving the woodlands themselves and fashioning a healthier environment for every living thing that ties itself to this and other similar, magically-watered canyons.

The witchery of color and light igniting the rock promontories, the wild and opposing combinations of desert thrift and wooded stream hem. The seductive incantation of these talking, tinseled waters, brings a potpourri of fish, bird, animal and plant that cannot exist without this wellspring. For beyond this wet sanctuary is nothing but a desert.

The spiritual implications for me are undeniable – a desert without an oasis is like a man without the Lord.

These remaining desert streams are spellbindingly beautiful and worth far more than money. Seeing is believing.

"Blessed is the man who trusts in the Lord, whose trust is the Lord.
He is like a tree planted by the water, that sends out
its roots by the stream, and does not fear when heat comes,
for its leaves remain green, and is not anxious in the year of drought,
for it does not cease to bear fruit."

– Jeremiah 17:7

Chapter 30:
Please Pardon Me Please

There's a field out there, I'm gonna walk it
A feelin' – easy... blowin' on the breeze
There's a field out there I'm gonna walk it
Pardon me please

There's a river somewhere cuttin' canyons
And with a boat... I'm gonna take her to the sea
Rivers roll and I'm bound to roam
It's bye-bye you're wavin' to me

There's a longin' that a sailor knows
That sets those ships to sea
A snow-goose sailin' when the seasons change
It's got to go... it's got to be
I've got that hobo-personality
I'm an explorer-extraordinaire
Yes, I'm that man
Yes, I'm that free
Please, pardon me please

There are mountains that climb into the heavens
A benediction this sojourner can't ignore

There are mountains out there... there's a river somewhere
There's a field out there... I'm gonna walk it
Pardon me please
Please, pardon me please
Please pardon me please.

From the tundra to the deserts to the wide-open sea
It's the story of creation callin' out to me
I love this livin' and the dreams they're for free
But you've got to chase them down to find a destiny.

San Pedro River

Chapter 31:
A River Sometimes Runs Through It

"There's a poetry about the lonely places and there are visions in the hills for those who have eyes to see."

– John C. Van Dyke

Life in San Manuel, Arizona is like the passing of geologic time – very little happens over long epics of chronological duration. The indefinite stretch of broad, brown desert, the distant, blue bordering mountains, the empty, azure sky, the anvil sun.

To the unobservant, these unadorned facts are undeniably true and seemingly unchanging. But the connoisseur by definition knows – love of the art lies in nuance, with the discriminating eye and the mind's ability to appreciate the subtleties that make up these simple truths.

Now long ago in the dreamtime, God made the world when no one was looking. Whenever this was accomplished, however long it took, it was a done deal. The earth, a kind of stage on which to play out His purpose and like a stage, as the narrative unfolds, things get moved around to help facilitate the telling of a good story. For mountains come and go. Oceans rise and fall. Sometimes it snows a lot. Sometimes it barely rains – too hot to handle sometimes, the sun. In a world where nothing stays the same, rest assured, nothing will.

The San Pedro River is the largest remaining, undammed river in the Southwest. It starts its flow in Sonora, Mexico and runs north down a protracted desert valley one-hundred-forty miles in length, before spilling its sometimes-running waters into the second greatest river in the west, the Gila. On the shoulders of this vast vale are a string of mountains, some approaching ten-thousand feet. The timbered tops of these celestial heights are adorned with ponderosa and Douglas fir forests filled with aspen, maple and deciduous oak.

As one descends these wooded worlds, it grows progressively hotter and dryer. Skyscraper firs give way to oak and piñon pine. Falling farther, growing warmer by degrees, these trees diminish in physical stature as forests begin to thin. Grass-lands advance, breaking the tree regiments, quilting open dells and meadows as the stunted evergreen chaparral relinquishes its position to an ever-pressing sun – thus abandoning any hope of standing against it. Even the mini-trees cower in the shadows. Ever-falling grassy slopes give way to plunging rocky desert aprons dressed in cactus, mesquite and palo verde that float like unspooling streamers to a magical river that receives almost no rain.

The age of the valley, ancient of days. It has seen many changes through time's long march. An ocean, long before the mountains pushed skyward, left the deposits of gypsum in the eroded badlands of today.

The mountains have been wearing away, at least as long as they have been standing. The deteriorating summits falling into the valley, debris sliding like rock glaciers off the giddy slopes and filling the sunken depressions with immeasurable amounts of stone. Hence, the valley's general architectural appearance: high wet wooded mountains with steep plunging slopes; long, waterless, declining desert ramps, falling into an immense, sunken river valley.

The scale of time required to whittle away mountains and carve this odd landscape is unfathomable, but one example may suffice. Alder canyon slides off the nine-thousand-foot crest of the Santa Catalina Mountains and runs to the San Pedro River some six miles distant. This small stream has cut a colossal canyon six-hundred feet deep and a half-mile wide, through the pure rock shoulders of the valley. Even though in times long past, this river basin received more rain than it does today, standing now on the cusps of this massive excavation, one knows well, this did not happen in a day or even a million years. Alder canyon was just one of many, forever-cutting canyons carrying away the cloud-capt belfry.

Once the stage was set, as it appears today – with the forested mountains standing proud, the sunken valley filling with debris, the river running through it – the general construction and look of the place, at least architecturally, has not apprecia-bly changed. Though the landscape is always changing and always will change, something a little closer to comprehensible in this metamorphic world is how the land dressed itself with appropriate apparel to meet the capricious weather changes that move across the land in any given block of time.

When the last ice age retreated, the land was cool and wet. Stone Age Clovis men hunted mastodon and ground sloth across verdant, grassy valleys interspersed with oak and pine and the river ran wide with rain. In the intervening centuries, it grew hot and dry. The persistent sun forced the trees to retreat to the mountaintop. Deserts stepped in to fill the vacuum with saguaros, palo verde and prickly pear.

This is where the nuance comes in, that is, where the trees and the cacti are growing. As the climate grew warmer and dryer, every living thing found a place where they could stand in the sun and be happy about it, or seek the perfect place to cower in a canyon's shadow, in order to take a stand against it.

From the Canadian environs at the tops of the mountains, to the Mexican environs at their feet, runs a full gamut of flora and fauna as wildly dissimilar as these two countries.

The forests climb down the sierra as far as they dare, and desert plants climb up until winter cold prevents ascension. By caprice of sun and shadow, at every step along the stair, there are plants living at odd intervals – making for a very interesting study and some startling revelations.

All I ever wanted to do is to write songs and take a walk somewhere. For a quarter century I have walked a great deal of Arizona and this river valley specifically. I have climbed to every mountaintop. Searched the deserts far below. Walked all the canyons. I know the placement of every tree and where all the anomalies endure.

I know of secreted maples, standing almost in the desert, but due to a lucky placement in the deep cleft of a certain canyon where shadows linger cool, they remain sequestered and segregated from their brethren by hundreds of years and thousands of feet. I know of the last remaining aspen tree, in a grove that stood for ten-thousand years, it too, soon to be a memory. Or where old growth forests of Douglas fir and ponderosa are lingering still, at unheard of elevations, due to the shear luck of the draw and the fall of a shadow. There is always a novel surprise and a startling new disclosure.

Anything that can eke out a living in this difficult land deserves the medal of honor because life in the desert is damn tough – and sometimes it's a whole lot harder than that. For starters, it never rains. In the summer, the sun is a death ray – like God, a consuming fire. Its heat puts the weight of the world on your shoulders. It robs the will. It takes lives. Death here is a way of life. Anything that remains animated and abiding has beaten the odds and when investigated, can teach natural and spiritual truth.

The valley is vast and empty. A great no-man's land and although others utilize these deserts, it appears I walk them by myself. It seems other people are busy doing other things. But I am a wanderer and a sojourner, a seeker of truth. I find it down by the river.

Now, I do not believe that nature made itself, or that I am the result of the whimsical serendipity borne by strands of DNA a billion years long. A house buildeth not itself, and nothing put together is assembled without love, through wisdom, for purpose and use.

I perceive landscape as a theater of spiritual operations and representations as well as natural ones. With the obvious and pronounced contrasts in this desert world, one need not unduly strain the imagination to perceive the spiritual beneath natural things placed on the surface.

A desert, represents "the absence of truth." Natural water, "spiritual truth" and rivers, "truth in abundance." "Come ye yourselves apart into a desert place, and rest awhile." Walk this desert and learn.

Water is the essence of a river and the San Pedro has precious little of it these days, at least water that flows on the surface. But there are a few segments along the river's course where water springs forth from the desert sands and the resulting oasis is nothing short of miracles and magic. For the sake of this essay, I shall concern myself with just a seven-mile stretch east of San Manuel and strive to tell of the shear joy I have had in exploring its shores for well over a decade.

Every young man needs a river and any river is river enough, the San Pedro River has been river enough for me. The anomaly of a stream that receives no rain that flows through a land that has no water is nothing short of spiritual revelation. Water is life – a desert has none. Life without water in the desert will not be for long. Learn the wisdom of rivers.

Keep in mind, the deserts that terrace above the river are vast and empty, peopled by saguaros. A landscape of rock and sediment, a wilderness of eroded crumbly cliffs with odd looking plants prepared to do battle with the unrelenting sun and do it with nary a drop of rain. The shear economy of the place – it is a stark earthscape and good for nothing in a practical sense. But it is rich in what it spiritually represents, a reservoir of truth, wisdom; aesthetic beauty for those who have eyes to see.

If you replaced the rocky landscape with water and froze it into its shape and form, it would be a vast ocean of undulating swells and breakers tossed and wind whipped. It is a theater where the play of sunlight and shadow reflects the color glory of a Sonoran sky ever-changing. There is always something to be discovered in the familiar lay of the land, as sunbeams cut through the cumulus and splash against a mountain range, loma, or canyon cleft, allowing the discerning eye a startling new facet never before detected. This change itself is but illusion, for the land changes not, as the sea does not change but the sky above it.

The land and the plants on it are changing little, though there are glory times like spring, when every plant has a flower. When out of nothing but rock, spring endless pastures of poppies in such profusion and proliferation, whole mountainsides appear gilded with gold. Or when hundreds of square miles of palo verde are a billion yellow balls on the land, fluorescent in the afterglow of a dazzling, desert day. After this flash-in-the-pan, the land slips in to sleep and waits for a good rain. But down by the river there is a different order to things.

Change along the river is on a daily basis. Things change so quickly that it is no surprise to be surprised – so much so as to not recognize where we're standing on the river banks; because just yesterday, or was it two years ago, or perhaps five, when the river flowed over here, or was it over there? A forest of cottonwood can appear out of nowhere and grow into a jungle of fifty-foot trees then, just as quickly, be swept away in the next big flood. Anything can happen and does happen and yet armed with that knowledge, I never cease to be amazed. Nothing stays the same. The commonwealth of life provided by the river's living waters; the river course itself and the valley through which it flows, everything tied to this peculiar place is in a constant state of flux.

The bed of the river is flat and wide with desert bluffs rising beyond. It is an amalgam of sand and fine sediments with a good amount of rock thrown into the mix. It is easily pushed around when floods roar, carving new channels at whim with each new rain. All the mountains – the whole of the valley of rock – is sliding like glacial ice into the river bottoms and pressing north. With a generous rain, incalculable tons of stone can sweep down a side drainage and change the river's course in less than an hour. The river can flow one-hundred yards wide, a full-fledged river with a good storm. When it doesn't rain, which is most of the time, its flow is but a crystalline brook of liquid life.

Out of nothing, from whence and where, waters spring to the surface. Out of nothing, life appears. In the arcing canopies of cottonwood and willow and the extensive mesquite bosques that line the river, half the avian species in the United States can be found working through the wood: eagles and ibis, mallards, vermilion flycatchers, great gray herons, Harris hawks and redtails, Orioles and Kingfishers. Ocelots and mountain lions and even occasional jaguars hunt unseen in the thickets.

The shock of spangled waters slinking over sand and gravel with little ponds and pools as clear as windowpanes where fish, frog and turtles ply their trade, leaves one standing stunned and disbelieving – even of that which is set before the eye. Beyond this linear oasis, are mountain views waving in the heat shimmer of a burning desert day where expanding landscapes wince under the sun's tyranny and not a drop of water can be found. The effervescent river is beauty, beauty, beauty and 100% glory.

There are occasions when there is so much bird life in the trees that it sounds like a tropical philharmonic of jungle calls with as much color as, well, red, yellow, and blue feathers floating and flashing through the green branches. Or, in turn, it can be as quiet as a church before service, when barely a breath of a breeze should hush the chorusing cottonwood that whispers of time and the ancient past.

In the glistening waters, there are thickets of bulrushes and cat-o-nine-tails; lining the shores, carpets of water-lettuce; grasses advance along the beaches, their seed tufts floating and waving like wheat fields with cocklebur forests arcing above them. Tall trees, in turn, arc above the river and a desert sky roofs it all.

The textures and the color contrasts, the intense blue sky, the cumulus clouds, the green of the wood or the gold of it in autumn, reflected in the lazy twists and turns of the river's flowing fountains, creates unending pleasure scenes and makes for a photographers paradise.

Through the years, I have taken it upon myself to chronicle the rivers changing moods, with inventories of stunning photos positioned at the same localities, throughout a season's turn. Every photograph completely different, nothing stays the same, always beautiful. Ever changing.

It is impossible to walk the river and not sense the weight of all that's gone before. The land is older than I can imagine and men have wended their way down the San Pedro beyond memory's reach. Wander up any side canyon off the river and find the evidence: Pictographs in caves recording the hunt, pottery shards cast among the creosote stands, prehistoric village foundations perched on the river bluffs, seven-hundred-year-old grinding mortars carved into black volcanic stone thirty-million-years-old, shaded by fifty-year-old cottonwoods, mesquite in the bosques a thousand years old and cedars on the hills as old as time – and all that time, men have walked the river.

The Spanish Conquistador Coronado marched his army down the valley in 1540, in a get-rich scheme of conquer and pillage. It would have all worked out, as planned, had they just found a city worth the taking. But it wasn't meant to be, though they found something almost as good – a gloryland in which to search for glory.

Father Kino wandered down the river in 1697, accompanied by Captain Cristobal Bernal and twenty-two Spanish soldiers. They were scared to death of the Apaches. It was fear well-founded. Fortunately, they met friendly Indians along the way, dressed in cotton clothes they grew and wove themselves.

James Ohio Pattie was the first American trapper and mountain man to enter Arizona in the 1830s. He called the San Pedro, "The Beaver River," for their prolific numbers made easy pickings.

The waterway was a highway through a desert land that could kill. Rather than face the formidable deserts to the west, the 49ers moved down the San Pedro till it spilled into the Gila River and followed it and their dreams to California gold.

Edward Shefflin found rich silver ore off the river eighty miles to the south and the story of Tombstone lives in infamy.

The Clovis mastodon hunters, the Hohokam and Anasazi, the Apache wars, the ranchers, the prospectors, the gunfighters, the Spanish Missions; it is impossible to walk the river and not feel the weight of all that's gone before – and all that's gone before is far more than we can know. For it happened long, long ago, in the dreamtime.

Now the river today, is not what it was, and what it is today, will not be what it will be tomorrow. The river has known nothing but change for a million years. Who can walk along its shores and not be touched by the glory of it, the wonder of it all – the tall blue mountains, the stark waterless desert, the animated river. Who cannot see that, when investigated spiritually, these natural things are correspondent and representative of deeper incorporeal things within our own selves and ultimately revealing the One who made it? Who cannot see, that this clear tumble of water is but a measure of spiritual truth? And is not my endless walking this river like a prayer?

*"I saw more than I can tell and I understood more than
I saw, for I was seeing in a sacred manner the shapes of all things
in the spirit, and the shape of all shapes
as they must live together like one being."*

*"Crazy Horse dreamed and went into a world
where there is nothing but the spirits of all things.
That is the real world that is behind this one,
and everything we see here, is like a shadow from that world
I knew the real was yonder, and the darkened dream of it was here."*

— Black Elk, *Lakota Sioux*

And so it is. The years have drifted by like a dream, endless days beneath the blazing hot sun. Countless evenings 'neath the diamond star ceiling. Innumerable sunsets standing in celestial light, where the sun's rays probe the land's contours like searchlights, glorifying every land-facet in polished shine and shadow. The prickly desert world a velvetized color dream. Where mountains gleam as molten metal and summer thunderheads glow like branding irons, pouring blue bannered blessings of water on the dry land.

And wisdom is the poetry in a river long run. The dreamtime's calling past into the present, where everything has changed and nothing has: The cottonwood's whisper, the willow's weep in the wind, the speechless nighthawks bobbing through the twilight, the peeping plover, the redtail's cry, the diamond-back's rattle. The lion's print and the bear's paw pressed in the sand where the silver waters braid. Where saguaros stand on the bleak bluffs and the song-dogs rendezvous, the scattering peccary, the bounding deer. The drifting herons wend above the river's sinuous curves.

The San Pedro is, by no means, the only beautiful river, but for me, the river closest at hand. If not this stream, another would be needed and sought out. The waterway has been a place to walk, to write to explore and drift into reverie. A place to relax the bow of my mind. I have logged hundreds upon hundreds of river miles and let those miles write my songs. Forgive me my dream. The San Pedro has become but a spiritual river road on my way to Damascus because I can't help but read the spiritual truth between the natural written lines on this

133

present page. This magical place is but a cinematograph through which I have let my feet and my mind wander.

Life in San Manuel, Arizona is like the passing of geologic time – very little happens over long epics of chronological duration. The indefinite stretch of broad, brown desert, the distant, blue, bordering mountains, the empty, azure sky, the anvil sun.

To the unobservant, these unadorned facts are undeniably true and seemingly unchanging. But a connoisseur by definition knows – love of the art lies in nuance, with a discriminating eye and the mind's ability to appreciate the subtleties that make up these simple truths.

Now long ago in the dreamtime, God made the world when no one was looking. Whenever this was accomplished, however long it took, it was a done deal – earth, a kind of stage on which to play out His purpose. Like a stage, as the narrative unfolds, things get moved around to help facilitate the telling of a good story. Mountains come and go. Oceans rise and fall. Sometimes it snows a lot. Sometimes it barely rains – too hot to handle, sometimes, the sun. In a world where nothing stays the same, rest assured nothing will.

I preach my best sermons while walking.
It is for certain that if I had written a sermon or a song
for every mile I've walked along the San Pedro River,
I'd have a catalogue you couldn't get through.
When I walk well, I think well, I write well, I preach well.

San Pedro River

Chapter 32:
In the Mornings of Home

It's an eddy in time
Where blue mountains climb and quiet canyons wait
Amorissa... down where the river goes
Wreathed in cottonwood groves

It's an eddy I find... for the heart and mind
For she loves and now she waits
Abides in dreams unawares... loves-light leading there

Bedouins and nomads... they know my freedom
These dreams like earnest prayers unanswered yet
Indefinite stretches I see... of desert and doubt for me
Till fortune favors my return... or in failure to atone
In the mornings of home

It's an eddy in time
Where blue mountains climb and quiet canyons wait
Amorissa... down where the river goes
Wreathed in cottonwood groves

Bedouins and nomads... they know my freedom
These dreams like earnest prayers unanswered yet
This desert I see... hastens return of this absentee
On the road a fool discerns... in hills not far I'll roam
Through the mornings of home... In the mornings of home
In the mornings of home

This is a favorite, for I love the sentiment in the lyric.
The scene, the San Pedro River valley –
I have an enduring affection for it.
And the running theme in much of my music:
despite our prized illusions and the impossible
dreams we can't make come true, in the end,
all we have of any real importance are the ones
we love in the mornings of home.

Chapter 33:
Along the Way

I'm a simple man with a simple dream
Just a misplaced Pennsylvania farm boy gone a wanderin'
And I walked me far from home
As I've shared the songs I heard along the way

Left the eastern forests green, southwestern desert bound
To walk the wild beyond the road to see what might be found
And I fell into a love grown true
With a landscape seen by few along the way

Along the way the mountains beckoned
Along the way the rivers sang
Along the way the distant valleys were ripped apart
And it so worked its magic

I guess a rich and famous tune-smith
Weren't born or bound to be
For my approach and theme for song perhaps anomaly
The psalms in the meadow like the dreams I see
Instill the joy that waits for me along the way

Along the way the mountains beckoned
Along the way the rivers sang
Along the way the distant valleys were ripped apart
And it so worked its magic

I'm a simple man with a simple dream
Just a misplaced Pennsylvania farm boy gone a wanderin'
And I walked me far from home
As I've shared the songs I heard along the way
Along the way... along the way.

I don't know anyone who has walked
as much of Arizona as myself
with the possible exception
of Charles Bowden.

Chapter 34:
Bobcats in Bonita

"To follow a creek is to seek a new acquaintance with life."

– Peter Steinhart / *The Making of a Creek*

 The Gila River tumbles out of New Mexico and cuts its way through Arizona's eastern mountains before spilling across the broad Gila Valley to water the cotton fields and the farming community of Safford. A dirt road skirts the waterway as it knifes through the Gila Box, a 29,000-acre National Riparian Conservation Area.

A small sign points the way to Bonita Creek. For miles, I climb up the waggly arcing hills that have muscled in on the river. The wrinkled landscape undulates, fluent mountainous drifts, canyonous furrowing folds between the rising ridges. Creosote springs from the stony ground and the sparse grass over the collective acres stains the gaunt uplands in delicate hues of olive and gold.

At the crest of the wave, I park my truck by a corral and peer off the brink. The flesh of the desert has been sliced wide open with the cutting blade still in the open wound, down the plunging slopes to the barranca floor and the tranquil stream, Bonita.

A four-wheel drive passage and the creek braid their way up the canyon. With my late arrival, (this is a day's walk, I've already driven 130 miles from Tucson). I have to march in as far as I can and be back before dark. The day is bejeweled and the walking easy.

Cambric stratus clouds gauze a blue sky and garnet-rock walls part like the biblical waters of the Red Sea. Mature cottonwoods mark time on wide gravel beaches and the summer cloak of skeletal sycamores crunch under foot. The sun streaming through occasional latticed canopies of walnut and the intonating musk of willow hangs in a hushed innocent air. Fish at my wading feet in a clear, crystal creek.

The Anasazi lived here centuries ago, the Apache after them, the latter (Geronimo and his cohorts) using Bonita as an escape route from San Carlos, when they would jump the reservation for their illegal Mexican forays. James Ohio Pattie, the first American trapper and mountain man to explore Arizona's beaver-rich rivers in the 1830s, is said to have attacked a grizzly bear in a cave in the canyon that darn near killed him. Today, Bonita is famed for its large raptor populations. I've come to watch the feathered predators fly the rim-rock.

After some miles, the red rock walls close in, restricting visibility. A layer of long-johns takes the chill off the shadowed hallway. The afternoon sun gilding canyon rims where creosote arms bob in the breeze and red-tail hawks patrol.

Life is a puzzle. Often I feel I'm the one piece that doesn't fit. Today I find my niche. Treading through the canyon at a fast clip in the usual euphoric state, this walking brings.

A resolute march of two and a half hours brings me to a large park where two extensive drainages enter the creek on either side, the valley planted with a mesquite bosque and well-spaced stratospheric sycamore and cottonwood. The creek is a vein of silver shining in the sun, a scarab of jade this planted garden, set in the cleft of the rounded rise of treeless hills. And on higher hills than these beyond, climb hunter-green milieus of piñon-pine that rune and wile and summon to beauties and mysteries that not this day nor a lifetime of exploration, unbosom or discern.

And for me... it's just the walking... walking... and this thought... I just might not return. Halfway back through the corridor a rock falls from a canyon wall. To my surprise, two big bobcats are coming down to the stream.

One stands on a ledge broadside with a stance like a show dog. I'm convinced they see me, but they keep climbing down. I step into a screen of desert-brooms in the hopes of seeing the cats cross the creek. Disappearing for a moment, I hear them crunching through the leaf litter and the green hedge-wall fringing the flow. A second later they walk out of the brush at my feet! Never looking up or giving any indication that they know I'm there.

I follow them down a crooked road for a quarter mile. With each bend, they're a little farther afield. With another turn, they're gone. Carefree and confident, princely and powerful, in their weight class, they're the kings of the jungle. I'm glad I'm not a rabbit in the neighborhood.

The day draws to a close. I huff and puff with the steep climb out of the canyon to catch the sun's consummating rays beaming over profiles of the Gila Mountains. On the shoulders of the canyon's eastern walls, Turtle Mountain stands naked in last light's blush.

Down the river rock slopes to the Gila, a green-gray ribbon twisting through the deepening lavender hills. I leave the water running and bobcats to hunt under a sliver of moon.

> *"We see the world piece by piece, as the sun, the moon,*
> *the animal, the tree; but the whole,*
> *of which these are the shining parts, is the soul."*
>
> – Ralph Waldo Emerson

Chapter 35:
I'm Just a Cowboy

The night is so pleasant when the moon shines bright
You'll see forever through a desert night
Halfway to Mexico...the Santa Ritas in sight
And I got lucky when I found a home
With all these open places here to roam
I climb the mountains high... I search the deserts below

I'm just a cowboy... I've got a song to sing
I feel the joy life brings as I ride across the plain
The sun and the rain... like a color-slide changin'
Bringin' motion to the land...like the changes the years bring
The feelin's that seem to spring
From where this cowboy takes his stand

I see the mountains standin' white in the winter
Shinin' wet when it rains
I see the Lord's work plainly... on a land stretchin' endlessly
And lately... I've got to walk somewhere... I've got to go

The days so pleasant and the summers long
A cowboy dreams of girls... a horse... a song
And a love he might find to share... singin' songs in the sun
If he's lucky... well, he'll find her there
Cool Senorita with the long dark hair
It's love deep that he'll find himself... under cottonwood trees

She's just a cowgirl... she's just a fool like me
She'd drive to Hart Prairie... just to say that she'd been there
She'd wait if she had too... for me on some barstool
I'm singin' longer than I planned
She brings a joy as the years go
Good lovin' that seems to flow
From where these cow-kids take their stand

I hope she sees me walkin' lonesome some canyon
Singin songs in her dreams
Cause I hear a song quite plainly... an endless melody
And lately... I've got to play somewhere

I'm just a cowboy... I've got a song to sing

I feel the joy life brings… as I ride across the plain
The sun and the rain… like a color-slide changin'
Bringin' motion to the land
Like the changes the years bring
The feelin's that seem to spring
From where this cowboy takes his stand

The night so pleasant when the moon shines bright .

*"I believe that all men are created equal and that every man
has within himself the power to make the world a better place."*

– The Lone Ranger's Creed

Ciénega Creek

Ciénega Creek

Chapter 36:
Ciénega Creek

"Loneliness, thy other name, thy one true synonym, is prairie."
– William A. Quayle / *The Prairie and the Sea*

So as to follow from a genesis, and in the company of well-springs abiding within foundations forming the Canelo (cinnamon-colored) Hills in southern Arizona, Ciénega Creek inaugurates a brief tenure, meandering north across the plains of Sonoita to the rising rhythms of a Rincon spire.

Now bordered on the east by the Whetstone Mountains and on the west by the Santa Ritas, lies a stunning sweep of seemingly endless prairie covering four-hundred square-miles of Montana-like grassland. Framed on all sides by grand, blue mountains whose forested slopes ooze onto the plain like syrup in the sun, to form the shore of an ocean of grass, that writhes and rolls where the wind wills. And calls the cowboy like a sailor, to ply his trade on the open waters.

Silver shafts of sunlight play on the shining sea of grass. Sculpted cumulus troop across the fathomless dome of blue, as the cloud shadows change the countenance of the mountains' proud profiles and with it the oscillating moods of the waist deep waters.

Along the bottom of this gigantic valley runs a tenuous tree-ribbon and a burbling stream. Its shores garland with cottonwood, walnut and willow, which decorates as it descends the vale perfectly and peacefully. This place is an Arizona scenic jewel, a rancher's nirvana; a cowboy's waking dream. Everyone's vision of what the west should be and ought to be. Within this valley and its bordering mountains, the history of the American west unfolded.

To the east, Coronado led a thousand men down the San Pedro River Valley in 1540, rummaging for golden cities; discovering nothing but disappointment. The very ground on which they walked housed millions in silver and 300 years later would produce the boomtowns of Tombstone and Harshaw. Money brought gunfighters, gamblers, the honest and the lawless.

To the west, Father Kino established his missions for God and King along the Santa Cruz River and opened the way for the trapper, miner, the rancher and the dreamer. They sought to explore and exploit whatever they could find for the taking.

The California 49ers drank from Ciénega's waters as they headed west for their imagined bonanza. The Butterfield Stage and the railroad crossed and trestled its course. The infamous Apache Wars all fought within and around its perimeters. A thousand stories told and untold, real and imagined, grew to legend in proportions commensurate to the size of this laudable landscape and lives in the hearts of every American to this day.

Much has and hasn't changed, ensuing the era of the Spanish explorers. Since the glory days of the 1800s, when a man with guts and a gun could test himself against the wilderness and with a little luck, come out not only with his life, but with money and a name.

Today the speculative prospector wears a coat and tie, and mines money from wealthy Easterners, who move to the burgeoning sunbelt-cities like Tucson in search of the good life. With Tucson bursting its borders just fifty miles to the north-west, any real estate developer worth his salt, sees Ciénega's fair valleys as something to be exploited as did former generations, but this time not with mining claims or cows, but with condos, shopping malls and golf courses.

As fate would have it or call it Divine Providence, the government has purchased the Empire Ciénega Creek Ranch, holdings of some fifty-thousand acres through the heart of the valley. In this way its ground water, measuring millions of acre-feet, might be saved for Tucson's future needs. That the endangered species of Gila Topminnow, that school in Ciénega's waters might be protected. To keep away the ruthless realtors who would sell their souls for a piece of the action. That this pristine portion of prairie-paradise might remain as it has since time began.

It is for certain that I am not a sailor and a cowboy only in spirit. I have set a course to walk the thirty-five-mile river, to see first hand, the Bureau of Land Management's purchase of

Ciénega Creek. To test myself against the landscape's colored contours and see what bounty the river possesses – to reckon summon and call.

Recruiting the services of my next door neighbors for the ride east from Tucson, the interstate flung us like a sling shot projectile, away from the confusion and chaos of the metropolitan morass. Away from the discontented city dwellers, cursing their lot and the evening traffic, to leave us free and flying across the creosote flats – big town distractions subsiding.

I point with excitement to the mountains that ring the horizon, now bold-blue blocks of color. The strange glow of the pink pastel desert floor, contrasting a gem-jeweled sapphire sky. The odd shapes of the luminous, opalescent-pearl-colored clouds. It is a typical evening in this southwest wonderland. They do not notice the beauty. I'm embarrassed that I brought it up. We talk of other things. The car rolls on. Charity attends an errand.

We arrive at the point where Ciénega Creek empties its waters into the Pantano Wash, unto deserts declining below. Here the river ends its northerly flow, and to a place the Rincon Mountains force the flood tides west, as the interstate intersects its course and continues eastward. The car pulls over, we say goodbye; they cruise back to Tucson. I am up a creek.

It's already late, as the sun hastens to end the day before I can put in too many miles. Stalking up the dry wash, I stumble over sere sand-shoals and congeries of river-rock. Soon the clouds are kindled to molten metal and a three-quarter moon helps extend twilight, letting me push on a bit farther. Just beyond a working ranch, now I won't be seen, I set up a tent. "Dinner for one."

Once, a few years ago, on another walk in the Whetstone Mountains, not terribly far from my present location, I came across a clutch of working cowboys complete with tents, fires, branding irons and very angry eyes. I was told to get out! Convinced they were going to start shooting, I want to avoid such confrontations.

I fall asleep under moonbeams with the doggies mooing and eighteen-wheelers whizzing down the interstate some miles off.

And the evening and the morning were the first day.

I open my eyes at dawn. After a breakfast of oatmeal and tea, I dismantle camp. I start up the dry river leaving the ranch and the cows behind.

Here the river's hemming wall scuttles just a few feet high. Low, shouldering desert hills cuddle wadis-silhouettes, embellished with ocotillo, creosote, mesquite and a good amount of grass. We've had a good monsoon this year and the desert blushes green.

The wash swings and sways, first this way and that. I try to walk as straight a line as possible, climbing up on the cobble-stone reefs and sand bars, forcing my way through the brush, then into the channel as it swings back around, wondering how far I'll go before welcomed water starts flowing.

I rejoice in the cool morning air, the baby-blue, cloudless sky, the new day's buttercup light, as it plays on the ocotillo arms that silently watch from the blunt bluffs above my head. Small birds work the undergrowth, apart from their singing and the crunch of gravel under my feet; there are no other sounds with the unfolding miles.

Quite unexpectedly, a small puddle with a few minnows. Not more than twenty yards up stream the river began flowing as though someone had turned on a spigot. At the water's edge where it disappeared into the sand, minnows swam and played. From that point on the river that prior to this was no river at all, it was suddenly a waterway filled with promise. I marvel at the fish, the surprising amount of water tumbling over the rocks on the wide, stream bed; noting the soothing voice of the waters as they made their descent and contemplated the spiritual implications of water flowing across a dry land.

> *"Remember not the former things, nor consider the things of old. Behold I am doing a new thing; now it springs forth, do you perceive it? I will make a way in the wilderness and rivers in the desert."*
>
> – Isaiah 43:18-19

I estimate my position at perhaps twelve indirect miles from the interstate. It's 10 A.M., and I'm already tired. Moving another half-furlong, crashing into the sand, breaking into the munchies: beef-sticks, candy and carrots, punctuated by great gulps of water. I take a few minutes rest, click a few photographs and inventory my surroundings.

Growth along the flood plain is thickening. Jungles of mesquite line the stream banks. Small walnut trees have appeared and willow bend their boughs and bower the flowing waters that beckon farther exploration. I strap on the backpack and stumble onward.

And going nowhere fast. The fount is forcing its way through low elongated parallel hills, forming 's' shapes and right angles. With each twist and turn, the rivulet has a differing disposition. In one place, the water is thirty-feet wide and two inches deep, or it's a trench three-feet wide and two-feet deep. Water is tumbling over rock shelves, gushing over gravel beds, or growing pockets of quicksand that impede my increasing labored steps.

Red-tailed hawks patrolling the sky. Squadrons of hummingbirds working the nearby flower beds. Yellow-breasted finches flashing from the treetops. Conventions of butterflies convening on the sand banks, some mating on the wing, in every color of the rainbow. Gigantic prehistoric-size dragonflies running reconnaissance missions along the water's edge as I walk awhile.

In 1961, H. Barnett, Ed Hilton, T. Ferguson, and S. Goodin shot and killed a jaguar, weighing 145 pounds, at the "Total Wreck Mine" in the Empire Mountains. This bonnie creek borders two miles and west. The predator was credited with consuming 20-25 calves, a yearling and a colt.

Espying a stream-side jaguar this day seems unlikely, but I'll keep my eyes pealed for the lion that left these tracks in Ciénega's sand.

An intense bright-beaming sun is burning the back of my neck, like an electric iron placed on permanent press, as I drag a ball and chain. I believe it to be a scientific principle: pack-weight, increases in direct proportion to the number of miles incurred. Shoulder straps are cutting like surgical blades through ham hocks.

A great gray heron spreads its silent wings and moves up stream, preferring to dine alone. I seek a siesta, the shade of a walnut tree, leisure and lunch.

The morning desert landscape falls away. After scaling a fifteen-foot waterfall, I step onto a rolling savanna, an emerald prairie. Grandiose cottonwood dot the flatland pastures. Oak and mesquite fill the seams on the rolling hills beyond. The 7,400-foot Whetstone Mountains form a bold backdrop, as the sky brews storm and thunderhead.

This is the last of the sweeping landscape I will see until the late afternoon hours. The runnel has bored its way through prairie sediments and carved a canyon ten-feet deep, from which there is no escape for myself, or the stream. Within its confines, I explore an inter-world of beauty. Flanking, swampy tributary bogs tangled-wood-arbors gorgeous and green as Borneo. I take guesses at whose tracks are pressed into the damp sands; delicate little hands and feet of javelina, coyotes or ringtail cats.

Time passing. Through the bends and the nooks, Ciénega Creek drags and drifts trickling lazily along.

I twig a great horned owl. His big eyes watch from a rotating head as I push my way through a patch of black-eyed-Susan below his perch. Then, with a boom of thunder the sky opens up. I welcome the rain and the rest, seeking shelter in a thicket of cottonwood.

For hours I have been marching. Approaching physical exhaustion. I sadistically enjoy the pain. I'm dirty, muddy, soaked to the skin – strangely content. Miles from nowhere and a kid in a candy shop. Beyond this valley rages an ugly city stuffed with people, with its concrete, cars, and "Circle K" convenience stores. I can scarcely believe that fact is true. Civilization is marching on without me. Delighted with the prospect.

The storm passes, pilaster sun shafts double down on the watercourse. Diamond raindrops sparkling, set the trees, the rocks and the grasses to glistening like a billion, buffed mirrors. I set out again through a steaming wet jungle. A few more turns and another mile, forthwith, I'm free of the river's prison walls.

Before me is the most idyllic ranch scene the mind could imagine. A gaucho's Kingdom Come. Under sky-azure-auras cumulus incandescent glow, bountiful fenced pastures, gigantic cottonwoods, blue-blobs, against gorgeous, green hills, that rise up one upon another like ocean swells, held in check by the bruised, forested peaks of the Santa Ritas and the Whetstones, miles distant. With the ranch houses, the barns and windmills, it's a pastoral tapestry that gladdens the eye; like a view across Jordan, virtues and visions of a promised Canaan.

A dirt road parallels the river, the ranch and beyond. I take advantage of the uncluttered path to find the ranch abandoned. This may be the Empire Ciénega Creek Ranch, but without a map, I cannot tell. Would anyone leave a place this well-proportioned and presentable? Perhaps they have been called, as unto Heaven.

Edward Nye Fish, Tucson businessman, established The Empire Ranch in the 1860s; a four-room adobe building on 160 acres. Walter L. Vail, a native of Liverpool, Nova Scotia, and Herbert Hislop, an Englishman acquired the spread in 1876. Walter proceeded over the next twenty years, as the west was being won, with the expansion of ranching, railroads, mining, and with various other partners, to enlarge his holdings to include over a million acres. A cattle-baron par excellence!

This verdant valley remaining in the Vail family enterprise until 1928. At that time, the title went to the Boice, Gates and Johnson partnership, successor to the Chiricahua Cattle Co. Frank Boice and his family, working the range and becoming sole owner in 1951 as the well-respected cattleman bred his famous Herefords till 1969.

The Ranch was sold off to a corporation, for a real estate development and later resold to a mining company that eyed the valley's mineral-wealth and water-riches. But as luck would have it, these aspirations came to naught and the BLM made a purchase; so for the present and foreseeable future, cows will remain kings on these gone-green dominions of demonstrative pasture. Which explains my being here, my standing in this scintillating sun, this obese backpack, and a need to press on.

The road turns west, I know not where. (The Empire Ranch House now a 22-room adobe and wood frame building dating back to 1870 and is listed in the National Register of Historic Places. It is nestling just up the road, hidden from my view, concealed in the lyrical cadence and climb of these emerald grassed hills.) I crash through the willow thickets and back into the water. The river is suddenly not a river at all. Stalled in a depression among the hills, I'm in the Florida Everglades.

With Herculean effort, I struggle through mud and muck to my knees. Trapped, like a mastodon in the La Brea Tar Pits. Clouds of mosquitoes move in for the kill. Scrambling to the shore, there is nothing but a wilderness of grass seven-feet tall and no escape. Headlines flash before my eyes:

**Unsuccessful songwriter found dead
in bizarre wilderness mishap.**

After thirty minutes, or an hour, or several lifetimes, I abscond the chains of the swamp, climbing up on some hills away from the mud and mosquitoes. There is a thunderstorm pouring over the Whetstone Mountains with the power of a nuclear blast. In a blowing gale, I set up the tent; the deluge begins.

I am totally spent and lie like a corpse and listen to the rain.

I take a walk after dinner upon my ridge above the river. There is a glory of color that rests upon this land, a beauty that passeth understanding that touches the spirit to wonder and worship. Brooding, dark-dim-Delphian clouds are throwing lightning bolts at the Whetstone Mountains and cobalt-blue curtains of rain are falling on its slopes, bringing out the colors in the rolling savanna so Emerald-Isle green, that it is permanently dyed into my memory. Not a landscape more perfect this side of Heaven.

> *"But ask now the beasts, and they shall teach thee;*
> *and the fowls of the air, and they shall tell thee:*
> *Or speak to the earth and it shall teach thee:*
> *and the fishes of the sea shall declare unto thee.*

Who knoweth not in all these that
the hand of the Lord hath wrought this? In whose hand
is the soul of every living thing, and the breath of all mankind"

– Job 12:7-10

And the evening and the morning were the second day.

In dawn's clear light, birds chorus rejoicing anthems –
portending promise and prophesied blessing. Across the
Elysian fields and rhythmical flow of hills, wreaths of clouds
hide the conifer forests of the Santa Ritas. Below me – a silver-
string of water, calling as an invocation. I decamp, as the
adventure continues.

Yesterday's swamp struggle is a bad dream. The river opens
up again and flows effortlessly across the grassland. With
unbridled enthusiasm, I splash through the morning under a
spell of inspiration. There is great beauty here. I am in love.
There are no words.

Another gray heron leaps from the willow canopy and
gracefully doubles back over the trees. Hawks are working the
skies above the range, killdeer the water's edge. Across the
fertile valley breathe, horizons of mountain and mist. I think of
the bear that call it home, of lions that leave peaks ragged and
torn to seek a kill on these plains below.

The price of admittance to this show is a physical test. Ciénega
Creek regains its high walls and a slow run. A marshy course
filled with bulrushes and water lily-like plants. I take turns
swimming through the soup, or forcing my way along the top,
where grass stands over my head. I startle a drove of deer
along the carved mini-cliff walls and they bound on spring-
boards into the thickets. One of Arizona's largest white-tailed
deer herds calls this valley home. If you can see them, you're a
taller man than me.

The river's flow, ends just as it began. Above a small puddle
teeming with minnows – nothing but a gravel bed. The spigot
is turned off, the flow stops at the tap and water is no more.

Morning miles have taken their toll. Out of gas, I lounge on
the sands, tank-up on sunflower seeds and snickers bars.
I relish the shade of a copious cottonwood and mourn the
death of the river.

I give the city not a thought. I drift into dreams. I ponder the big questions; the ones past finding out, the wonder of it all. My ignorance is bliss.

Ciénega Creek is a dry wash now. A driveway of smooth gravel banked by lush green grass. Roadrunners dart to and fro, quail like shotgun blasts, explode from the olivine borders. The cottonwood and mesquite that peppered and seasoned the savanna along the way disappear completely with the miles. A Nebraskan prairie rolls on as far as the eye can see.

So, growing weary of the wash's confines and sensing the direction I should go, I set a course across the mantle of grass. There is great freedom in open spaces like these. I fly and float, drift effortlessly across the grass gardens like the cumulus clouds aloft. The belittling proportion and sweep of the champaign turf-realms, curry and coddle, inundate and engulf; inculcation under a marvelous light and the rolling ridges change their moods with the sky. The afternoon and the miles go by. The distance done.

The U.S. Boundary Surveying Commission, led by John Bartlet, sailed this sea and canvassed the valley in 1852, describing these undulating savannas as similar to the "western prairies." In the depressions of the dale were pools of water, luxuriant grasses and groves of small oaks. A herd of wild horses were spied, deer and antelope frequently seen. Col. James Graham, an accompanying member of the survey-ing contingent reported a great many antelope grazing and commented on this greensward glen, bordered by the Whet-stone Mountains on the east and the Santa Ritas on the west.

"This whole valley was covered with the most luxuriant grasses
we had anywhere seen. Our mules fed upon it as they traveled,
for it was from 3-4 feet high in many places...
We encamped in the valley, without water.
The grass was, however, so green and fresh
that our mules did not appear to suffer...
We were obliged to keep close to the southern margin of the valley,
because it began to be quite boggy in the middle."

I am crossing an Arizona Serengeti, Mt. Wrightson, the 9,400-foot summit of the Santa Ritas Mountains, a Kilimanjaro.

152

I search the dewy-downs for elephants and wildebeest, but the only thing that's moving are some cattle on distant hills, the grass at my feet, clouds whizzing overhead. And the pronghorn antelope that graze this grass are sailing some other quadrant of this chrysolite sea.

"There is no describing the prairies. They are like the ocean in more ways than one, but in none more than this: the utter impossibility of producing any just impression of them by description. They inspire feelings so unique, so distinct from anything else, so powerful, yet vague and indefinite, as to defy description, while they invite the attempt."

– John C. Van Tramp / *Prairie and Rocky Mountain Adventures*

In the late afternoon, I set up camp about a mile and a half from Route 82, a road running west from the small city of Sierra Vista beyond this valley, to the tiny community of Sonoita, set upon the hill from which Ciénega Creek starts its flow. My journey is soon over.

Dinner is enjoyed in the bright light of a sun shower, the eastern sky a dyestuff color-curtain of ebony and indigo, as double-arc semicircle rainbows frame the enkindling grassland buttes, in Ansel Adam visions of Wyoming.

After my meal, I walk the rolling swells and flowering prairie glades transfixed by the pageantry and power of a thunderstorm as it terrorized polished purple magisterial peaks, flung faraway and climbing, clothed in blue cumulus and lightning. Sunbeams, like searchlights, punched and poured through the cloud holes, solid as rays of steel. In places such as this, I'm convinced there are no disbelievers.

In the deepening-blue vesperal shadows of twilight, I hear the thunder of hooves. Up over a rise not twenty feet away at first, fly fifteen pronghorn and the feeling is rapturous. Here is an animal that looks like it stepped off the African plain, but these mercurial creatures are an American-original. Antelope have roamed this valley since time began, designed to wander far and free, to scamper and skip, sprinting quicksilver zip, or stand quietly for uninvited guests. A primeval experience; humbled and honored to be in their presence. A full moon lights the prairie dancing.

And the evening and the morning were the third day.

At sunup, I walk the final few miles across the prairie.
Observing the last twists and turns of dry Ciénega Creek as it
makes its way to its inceptions, a bantam basin in the graceful
grassy ascending-lilts abutting the oak-crowned Canelo Hills.
In the small town of Sonoita, I stick out my thumb and catch a
ride back to civilization – abetting a wayfarer's woe.

Though man has traversed the valley since time immemorial, I
know of no one who has walked the length of this river. These
days, it is not on the itinerary of things people aspire to do. I will
cherish the accomplishment.

Tucson is as I left it. Cars crowd the ugly streets. Drivers
jockey for pointless position at the traffic lights. Myriads mill
in the markets and malls. The city, like a cancer, grows. And a
sun sets, and a moon rises, and the good life in the fast lane –
hastens on.

I can't help but think, if the earth is our mother, we have
broken the fourth commandment.

And the evening and the morning were the fourth day.

I have drunk deep from Ciénega's waters and the brazen-
beauty of the valley and in walking through it, have
participated with and become one with the enchanted
landscape. It is locked into all my senses. Hopelessly
infatuated with the glory of it all, this love is a thing
experienced, not rationally explained.

The Bureau of Land Management's purchase of the Empire
Ciénega Creek Ranch, is an act I wholeheartedly approve.
I know a good buy when I see one. It's comforting to know
that in a world where 20th century man consumes wild places
like he does fast food, this river valley will be protected.
Life will continue as it has, since the day the Lord set this
sphere to spinning along a watercourse called Ciénega.

> *Go hang a sliver of moon in the dawn of a western sky*
> *Let the road run long… khaki-colored prairies wide*
> *Set mountain row on row… and there I go again.*

Ciénega Creek Rail

The Galiuro Mountains

Chapter 37:
Mountain Songs

I never understood the city
Why anyone would choose to stay

Soon, the mountains will be rising
From a plain grand and sweeping
Standing high where the snow's rarely gone
Far above the trees there standing
Lies the tundra cold but handing-over streams
Now, they're starting to flow
Cutting deep the tortured canyon course
A siren-song that calls and forces me to climb and see
It's of color, space, and time astounding
Pastures, forests, skies abounding

You know I believe… in mountain songs
You can't be down for long with a mountain song
Give up those city throngs for a mountain song

Now, there's something in the wilderness
For me there's no describing
On the trail, those urban-blues are gone
It's the wonder in the canyons glowing
Freedom in a storm that's growing
Joy in those stars at the end of a day

I know a peace… the favored streams I walk
The Lord I hear when nature's talking
His hand in all I see
My heart a song in praise to all its glory
Until the day the Lord should call me

You know where I'll be… singing mountain songs

I never understood the city
Why anyone would choose to stay
There's nothing in those streets but trouble
When it's trouble you find… go ease your mind with a song.

Pipestem Canyon

Chapter 38:
Pipestem Canyon

*"The glittering treasure you are hunting for day and night
lies buried on the other side of that hill yonder."*

– B. Traven / *The Treasure of The Sierra Madre*

The Mercer ranch rests in a small valley behind Sombrero
Butte and the western walls of the Galiuro Mountains.
A mining road lances up the slopes as I inch along beneath the
wincing weight of a backpack. Make a vow; I will never carry
water again.

In less than two miles, there are blisters on my heels the size
of half-dollars. I've walked a thousand miles of primitive
Arizona, no problem. Today there's a new rub. The damage
done, mole-skins provide an ineffective veneer against
increased pain and suffering.

I leave the road maneuvering up a sharp rock face crowded
with brush and runt oak, then ardently inclining open slopes
to the mountains' crown. A twenty-two hundred-foot climb
and a pleasant walk, but with a backpack, it's the hardest
thing I've ever done.

From the summit stones the 10,700-foot Pinaleño Mountains,
beyond this range to the east, are a distant blue wall with a
mantel of white. The tip-top of the crinkle I've climbed drops
like a banner into Four-Mile-Creek, a ribbon of green oak and
blue juniper working down the drainage. The foreground, a
crumpled-quilt of stony grass slopes tossed and tumbling afar
into Aravaipa Canyon and gill. With wild woods retreating into
shaded dells where even at six-thousand feet, the sun sternly
defines their borders barred. To the west, the San Pedro River,
an imposing empty turn-valley, minus the mining community
of San Manuel and the far-off ken climes of the Santa Catalina
Mountains.

Ride the arcing back of the mountain, dropping over the other
side and engaging the headwaters of Pipestem Canyon.

I walk an ancient landscape. Yesterday in Tucson they found

the bones of a dead man three-thousand years old in the side of a riverbank. Seven-thousand years before his death, Stone Age Clovis Men were hassled, hunting mastodon in the valley below.

Arizona was cool and wet back then. In the intervening centuries, it grew hot and dry. The sun replacing the trees with cacti while forests retreated to the mountains' meridian, climbing into elevated canyons where a desert sun would not fall. Noting where trees grow here is always an interesting study.

The canyon is a golden trough of grass hills without a tree, but in the seams, a generous oak-forest where trees stand thirty-feet tall. In the distance a small pocket of pine, standing in the shadowed cleft of Rhodes Peak, a harbinger of wonderful discoveries to come.

I shuffle down the canting coulee under a green canopy, breaking onto a terrace above the trees and the stream, startling deer that disappear as quickly as they are seen.

I'm mad at myself for carrying this much water with this much present. The last two days of rain have filled the rivulets with a gush. The burden I carry requires all I have. The hillsides are platinum blond roofs; the trees in the drainages grow in the gutters. Silvered waters are tumbling down these roofs and the gutters are rattling.

Drop into a tributary rill and deposit my pack in a cove of heroic cedars and nearly float into the air freed from the weight. I leave my cross where it is and explore the neighborhood.

Hobble the canyons' pitching path, crippled by the blisters, looking for a possible campsite. The ravine drops stiffly and is crammed with oaks and junipers, a maple or two, further down the Chihuahua pine. Afternoon sun streaming through jungle branches. Water tumbling over rocks with a roar.

Wander up the Crest Trail, I climb two-hundred feet to a bald plateau, perfect staging for my explorations. From here, I can look up the canyon from whence I came, down the extensive canyon I hope to go, the path that leads to Rhodes is at my door.

Set up camp, gather wood, climb a ridge to watch the sun go

down. With the last light, I look across the broken ledges of the Galiuros. This much wilderness makes me realize how much I'm committed and how alone I really am.

Beyond the fire's glow, the night is nothing but darkness and the distant flicker of innumerable stars, with a moon-crook finale.

With the morning, I'm a centenarian. The day's course is along the Crest Trail. Rhodes Peak is a cap of rock and the high point on this rift and ridge. An acre of scraggly ponderosa pines linger in its shadowed northern exposures. Beyond this 7,100-foot mountaintop, where the sun presses hard, stunted oak and piñon pine, with tight tangles of manzanita tumbling precipitously into deep-seamed canyons where wonderfully, at five-thousand feet, there are stands of Douglas fir.

These mountains are a hinterland as truly defined. No roads, no people, rarely visited. The official wilderness is some 76,000 acres but this is attached to an uninhabited chunk of rugged real estate the size of Rhode Island. The Sierra Club describes this landscape as primeval in character as any in the United States. When you wander in, you wander alone – the big lonesome and then some.

The land is so infrequently traveled that trails are almost nonexistent. You walk along sensing a path of faintest impressions. I follow along for miles, puzzle the trace, as far as I perceive it going. Turn around where the manikin forest topples off the western escarpment.

Take my time on the way back, watching over the stern landscapes blue corrugations.

Completely spent from the riggers of the last two days. In the amphitheater where I find myself camped, stretch out beside the tent, beneath the roofing arms of a huge and haughty alligator juniper- in sunlight so intense, Heaven's light could not be brighter. It's windy and the grassy slopes breathe with the warm air. I melt as butter in a heated pan. I wonder whether it's a loss of strength or will, but it matters not; lying down is all I can muster.

After a rest, I limp about gathering more wood. The blisters have ruined me. Up the golden hillsides to watch the sunset.

Down the hill through the twilight for dinner, a fire, the moon.

I'm just a shadow with the morning. The best of the walk, ahead. Pipestem drops steadily four-to-five miles down into Rattlesnake Canyon through a forest of mixed conifer, wonderful to behold. The Galiuro Mountains are filled with anomalies of vegetation at unaccustomed elevations. Old growth stands of ponderosa line the canyon floor. I can't think of another timberland of this caliber and this low, anywhere else in southern Arizona. Small pockets of isolated trees hiding in the clefts of secluded ridges.

To walk these woodlands is to walk in the spirit. I marvel at creation and the aura of peace that forests exude. Big blobs of bear scat as I press through the understory. Oaks, cedars, yucca, maples, ponderosa, Douglas fir, agave and sycamore; wonderful collections these intricate gardens.

The miles unfold in a serpentine fashion and Pipestem spills into Rattlesnake. Lunch at the confluence, gaining some strength and proceeding up the main drag.

Water flows free over a wide stream bed. The canyon planted like a garden. Wide open shelves beside the river. Wonderful esthetic tree groupings. A landscape artist could find his muse here and if he could capture its forlorn and haunt, he would be a master craftsman.

I'm in the heart of a vast chunk of wilderness, in the mist of topography so difficult, a virtual fortress against the outside world. Few scale its walls to plunder these visual treasures. It is a place separated by more than just its cumbersome configuration and the physical distance one can measure to civilization. A less definable line, is the mystery that enshrouds landscapes like these; we need feral places like this. It reminds us, that the world is a place that we do and don't know any-thing about.

In the thickets, deer appear. They graze, they love and the pedigrees continue. Through the hot summers, bears forage and their cubs learn the ropes; in winter they can't stay awake. A lion leaps from the shadows and a deer is missing from the drove. A bighorn guards the rock-ridge. Proud-pronghorn, prance the prairie. "With the Lord one day is as a thousand

162

years, and a thousand years as one day." And so it seems, no one knows and no one sees.

Beyond these mountains, deserts expand under the weight of huge cities. People drive their cars, live out their lives in comfortable houses, in ever-expanding convenience and technology. Neither denizen of either world knows of the other or scarcely comprehends. I don't comprehend. Though man there, has been distracted and this primitive world remains. It's nice to know there are still unattended land-scapes, places this magnanimous, secret and imposing, there-fore to woo and wade and wander.

A half-mile up Rattlesnake Canyon the water stops flowing. A driveway of smooth sand runs for miles up to Powers Gar-den and beyond. Bonnie and bone dry. This intaglio is big, an insular watershed of perhaps 140 square miles, but try and find some water. To sojourn there, you'll have to walk and climb. It's the only way. Accomplished with sweat and strain and damned hard work. Apart from the intimidating size of this back country, and the unaccommodating topography, water is as hard to find as gold and worth considerably more. Come summer when it's over a hundred degrees, a man that comes unprepared can find himself in big trouble.

I've had a few chancy close calls in these mountains, when it's very hot and dry and completely devoid of any rescuing-water. These life-threatening distances can be longer than one can possibly imagine. In requisites so arid and dire, "giving up the ghost" has more appeal then the fight; or is it, "better the devil, you know."

A golden eagle lifts off a deer carcass thirty paces to my left and flies at chest level through the trees toward me, but slightly ahead. With a determined step, I could have caught it as an incoming pass, though it was considerably larger than persnickety, diminutive me.

Later in the afternoon, I retraced my footsteps, under a tree came the strangest of sounds, a rush of air indescribable. Not a swish or flap of wings, but a continual wash of air as from a fan, or the singing edges of a wind-tunnel. Had I not seen the same eagle rising above the treetops, I could not have imagined what could have produced such a hearing.

Accosted by two red-tail hawks, the regal raptor, before he could gain any real lift and certainly any speed, being inches from the canopy, with a seven-foot wing span, did a 180-degree flip. Its talons straight away skyward in defense. Then a pure pirouette with the ease and dispatch of a flicking wrist, before it disappeared above the lattice of tree branches.

I make a side excursion and thread through Mailbox Canyon – more wonderful woodlands, disquieting and lonesome. There are Douglas fir in these Gothic mountains ancient of days, oracles worthy of Druid worship: wisdom, beauty, intelligence personified. Sequestered pockets of pine lingering in the shadows. How many centuries have they stood alone in canyons unvisited?

> *"Generations pass while some tree stands,*
> *and old families last not three oaks."*
>
> – Thomas Browne

> *"There is a relation of all things of the created universe to man.*
> *In the spiritual world this is seen clearly. In that world, also, there*
> *are things of the three kingdoms (animal, vegetable, mineral) and in*
> *the midst of them the angel; he sees them about him,*
> *and also knows that they are representations of himself; yea,*
> *when the inmost of his understanding is opened*
> *he recognizes himself in them, and sees his image in them,*
> *hardly otherwise than as in a mirror."*
>
> – Emanuel Swedenborg

The long return is uneventful with this exception. I've an uncanny memory when it comes to landscapes and getting disoriented is a rarity, but it can happen. The last few miles of my journey, a rue and woe. I don't recognize where I am!

Three days ago, when I entered these mountains, water flowed from every seam. Now, the volume has been reduced in these canyons by more than half and so changed the look of the place that it's abruptly unfamiliar. I am tired. I trudged the whole day long. It's growing dark. I walk for a half-hour in terrible uncertainty. Finally, I find a pool of water that I'm sure of and the sense of relief is profound.

To walk a distance in the city, you give it not a thought. At the end of a day in the wilderness, you think of the miles beautiful and empty; the space you alone have crossed. It's a little scary and equivalent to a metaphoric walk of faith. The Good Shepherd is attentive to sheep wandered from the fold.

The night is a tunnel, with a light at both ends. Dinner and a fire, the moon for a friend, a dream for the morrow... loves dividend.

I rise leisurely with the morning and disassemble camp at the same pace, blisters and sore muscles, governor gunning the engines.

Climbing out of Pipestem Canyon in more glorious sunshine. Up the green gutters beneath thirty-foot trees, over arcing golden roofs, down slant-steep chaparral slopes to a waiting ranch and a butte named Sombrero.

Exhausted, knocking on the door, Linda welcomes me home. She's just started there as caretaker and is busy painting interior walls, sprucing up the place after years without a woman's touch; glad for a break and I, for a soft chair and rest.

A report on the landscapes traversed, of the noble pine forests that lay hidden beyond these desert ridges, of which she knows nothing and can scarcely believe, even though she's been a San Manuel resident for years.

We are buddies. In an hour we cover lots of conversational ground, though a more exquisite repose, awaits me at home. I say goodbye, thanking her for letting me park the truck at the ranch and leave her a tape of some of my songs. Against the odds, she wishes me success.

I climb mountains; anything is possible.

"The symbolic and religious significance
of mountains is endless."

– Mircea Eliade

Snow in the High Country

Chapter 39:
Snow in the High Country

I hear the crash of falling cataracts
Like the roar of distant waves
It's talking through cold canyons curling
Come see what storms and mountains make
To the snow in the high country

I see the bend in a wild river running there
Across an endless stretching prairie gone green
Blue-mountains like fences rise up as great stone stairs
That's the view from my front porch screen
To the snow in the high country

Dreamers do what dreamers must
Pride will whip you all the way
Love has to work at something
Head and heart construct a way
My gift is in the singing... my gift is with a song
But through the fortnights when I'm fading
When the miles and days are long... I close my eyes

To hear the crash of falling cataracts
As they carve a colored canyon still untamed
My dreams are west of that hundred meridian
That's where this wanderer's heart remains
To the snow in the high country

Snow in the high country.

My tent is strategically placed at the confluence of two small crystal streams with fish darting to and fro in the singing flashing dancing water. Sitting at the forest edge, I look across a broad-sloped clearing at the bottom of Ash Creek Canyon in the 10,700-foot Pinaleño Mountains in southeastern Arizona. A wall of spruce is charging up the opposite side of the canyon. The ridge, rolling and sweeping like an ocean swell unto the lofty peaks of the high country, all dyed in a blinding blue. Hundreds of butterflies are working the foreground meadow flowers and the flurry of motion, as the sun plays on their wings, produces a twinkling constellation of yellow stars across the green firmament.

The day is perfectly still, not a breath of air, nor the slightest sound but my hammering hydrant-heart and the blood swishing past my ears. There is a crashing through the brush when unawares, a bear steps out of the wood standing still in the silent sun. We watch each other, rather cautiously, for a few minutes. He makes a broad semi-circle around me, noting my presence but not being overly concerned. Then with a blink of an eye, he flies like an arrow shot through the trees. Gone. I cannot get the blue of that spruce forest or vision of that bear out of my mind.

In the gathering twilight of an August evening I sit enthroned on the crest of a prestigious swell of rolling prairie in the middle of the Sonoiton-plain. A herd of pronghorn antelope thunder up the ridge and screech to a halt, as quick as they came, and proceed to stare me down in the darkening dusk as the moon lights the prairie dancing.

This is the culmination of a thirty-five mile walk up Ciénega Creek, across a stunning landscape of verdant expansive grass hemmed in by bold blue-mountains. I have basked in the sun, fought thunderstorms and gale force winds. I've splashed through the water, marched through the mud. Menaced by mosquitoes and physical fatigue. I am nearly exhausted, but I've never felt more alive. I cannot get the green of those savannas or the picture of those antelope out of my mind.

Pewter-colored clouds are strewn across a cold and threatening February sky as I make my way across the wide brown, grassy expanse of Sulfur Springs Valley. Antelope stand watching as I enter High Creek Canyon, an eastern gate to the Galiuro Wilderness and a thousand square-miles of the big lonesome.

My progress by fits and starts, as I labor up steep slopes. Gray roofing nimbuses. The air at times filled with snow flurries, the afternoon crisp and embracing, bordering on very cold. What the hell am I doing here? I continue to climb.

The Galiuros are wild and woolly, though not very high compared to the Santa Catalina Mountains or the towering Pinaleños that stand on ether side of its broad valleys. You might consider them no real mountains at all. But you'll change your mind should you wander into them.

In the hot southwest, one doesn't encounter serious conifer forests before ascending to elevations above six-thousand feet. Pines like cool, northern slopes where they can hide from the oppressive sun. The Galiuros can't even make eight-thousand feet with its highest reach and most of its ridges float along comfortably a thousand feet below that. But the acute architecture of these forlorn mountains is so deeply faceted with canyons, that ancient fur forests cling like flies to its shadowy perpendicular walls, while the mountaintops, have nary a pine. The place has a lonesome primeval look about it that can make your hair stand on end, but there is little to fear except winter's cold.

Reaching the near summits I swing over to northern exposures and wander through the big trees and snow banks knee deep. This is my first time across this mountain pass (though it will not be my last) I come equipped with a map, but with the snow's depth increasing, I can't actually tell where to go as I sense my way across the deepening snow-fields.

The day's walk culminates at the apex of a narrow, mountain ridge that divides the head waters of Paddy's River to my right and Rattlesnake Canyon to my left, as it plunges two-thousand feet on either side. Along the backbone of this divide – a whole mountain unto itself within a series of mountains – I set up a tent on stony ground. I grope for firewood that would become my salvation from a night brutally cold and watch the sun go down in a blaze of glory behind the Santa Catalina Mountains and the wide San Pedro River Valley.

I do not like the cold even though I have reluctantly spent my share of numbing nights in the wilds. I am sure that arctic winters are not one degree colder than the temperatures measured that crystalline night in the Galiuros.

Long before the sun went down, I could see my breath in long smoky columns. My shivers and shakes unmitigated with layers of long johns and hooded sweatshirts, that grew into body tremors so strong, I could barely work flesh and bone at all. A stiff wind poured up and over the mountaintop that imprisoned me along a roaring fire's perimeter till dawn. If I hadn't a fire, I would surely have succumbed. With the morning, my water jugs were frozen block solid. I defrosted a few chipped chunks for coffee and crumpets, using that to resurrect iced appendages.

James Ohio Pattie was the first of a hand-full of white trappers and mountain men to explore Arizona, wandering the Gila and the San Pedro rivers in search of beaver. On March 30, 1833, with his horses and most of his provisions as well stolen by Indians, he quit the San Pedro with a small party of disheveled vagabonds and struck eastward. They hoped to reach the Gila River and eventually get back to the copper mines of Silver City, New Mexico, from whence they came. Upon leaving the river, the hunting party had to climb some high mountains, it was the Galiuros – where I spend this frozen night. He reported, *"Met no traces of game."*

Stumbling out of the mountains on April 2, Pattie recounted: *"In descending from the icy mountains, we were surprised to find how warm it was on the plains. On reaching them, I killed an antelope, of which we drank the warm blood… Tasting like fresh milk."*

The Galiuro Mountains in the winter are as lonely and as cold today as they were in the 1830s. Though it may be hard to distinguish fact from fiction in the accounts of Mr. Pattie's rowdy exploits, I suspect there is a lot more honest truth than hyperbole. But of one thing I am certain. He described these

170

rugged frigid Galiuro peaks as the *"icy mountains."* This is clear, concise, accurate reporting.

Emancipated as I was from the paralyzing cold of the night, as eager as I thought myself to continue exploring, peering off the steep precipice from which I stood – the plunging slopes filled with deep snow; the rugged, belittling landscape stretching out before me, myself, its only inhabitant; the physical demands already experienced; and knowing what it might take to reach my intended destination – I could not convince myself to move one step forward. I wisely humbled myself before the *"icy mountains,"* and admitted defeat.

I cannot shake the cold of those mountains from my bones. I cannot get the vision of that high, lonesome landscape or the gleaming white of those frozen snow-fields out of my mind.

The effective finger-picking pattern through
the open airy chords of "Snow In the High Country"
leaves the listener conjuring a silent snow falling through
its imploring melody. But the voiceless storm is passing,
and the last few flakes are floating to the ground so the
melody ends as the snow began in whispering cold and cloud.

On the Road to Zion

Chapter 40:
On the Road to Zion

On the road to Zion
The Gila runs with the Mescals risin'
Big blue skies and I'm on the road to Zion

On the road to Zion
Broad deserts and pasture lands
Climb to forest stands I'm on the road to Zion

There's a world beyond my little world
A bigger dream beyond this horizon
There's a world beyond my little world
That's what I keep my eye on

On the road to Zion
Bright tumbling streams that run
Off the Mongollon
I'm on the road to Zion

It's a call on Canaan land… where a Jordan flows
Through tabernacled canyons… basilicas like Rome
Searching pilgrims come… for the New Jerusalem
And to scan the view… now look how far I've come

On the road to Zion
Past the peaks to climb stairs
This stone… small and alone
I'm on the road to Zion

There's a world beyond my little world
A bigger dream beyond this horizon
There's a world beyond my little world
That's what I keep my eye on

On the road to Zion
Deep canyons and the Kaibab risin'
Big blue skies and
I'm on the road to Zion

There's a world beyond my little world.

*"For the Lord will comfort Zion; He will comfort
all her waste places, and will make her wilderness like Eden,
her desert like the garden of the Lord; joy and gladness
will be found in her, thanksgiving and the voice of song."*
— Isaiah 51:3

There are two temperatures in Arizona: Too damn hot, or too damn cold; and it seems, almost nothing in between. The Sonoran Desert has two rainy seasons, summer and winter and in between those two time-slots no rain at all. June is our hottest and driest month of the year, the "death-watch" before the long awaited monsoon rains appear. "Hell hath no fury like a woman scorned" – or the savage deadly weight of our steamroller sun. This is the time to get out of town if at all possible. I'm on the road to Zion.

Utah is a spectacular state and has some of the most varied scenery in the West. Celebrated Arizona writer, Edward Abby, thought the whole place should be set aside as a National Monument. Of course, making something a National Park is the very last thing one should ever seriously consider, for it brings far too many people. But I cannot envision a natural landscape more appropriately fashioned for the Mormon's spiritual vision of the New Jerusalem, nor contemplate a more strikingly impressive location worthy of such an exalted status – and I might add, more appropriately named – than is Zion National Park.

I like, as a running theme, in my song writing a spiritual double-entendre. *"On The Road To Zion,"* on its face, concerns the 500-plus mile drive from San Manuel, Arizona to Zion, Utah. Those familiar with the lay of the land will recognize specific landmarks going by, The Gila River and The Mescal Mountains, The Mongollon Rim, The San Francisco Peaks near Flagstaff, The Vermillion Cliffs, and The Kaibab Plateau. But as with most things worthy, there is more to this than meets the eye.

The natural Zion is representative of our spiritual home distant this one. "The world beyond my little world, a bigger dream beyond this horizon," is obviously Heaven.

The very act of walking and traveling across landscapes is analogous to a walk of life with profound spiritual implications. As plodding pilgrims we journey by unseen providential hand toward our ultimate eternal goals. This is why landscapes hold a great deal of weight for me, because I see natural things as correspondingly representative of deeper spiritual realities. Walking through spectacular natural canyons, who does not perceive spectacular spiritual cathedrals and think of the promised glory that waits the faithful who put their vested trust in the Lord our God? These tangible truths and actualities are the everlasting shores for which I hope to have set my course and trimmed my sail.

Listen and hear nature sing. Tall mountain turrets
like church steeples ring. Call this believer there
to wandering through splendid hues of stained-glassed skies.

"To walk in the land of Israel is a holy thing to do."
— Bruce Feiler

"One who is able to reflect wisely will very clearly notice that
the heavenly paradise is represented in the earthly one, and
that from this all things in nature bear relation to such as are
in the spiritual world. And one who
is able to draw further conclusions will perceive that
nature does not subsist from itself, but through influx from
heaven, that is, from the divine in heaven; insomuch that if the
communication were taken away, all things of earth would fall
down to nothing. That this is so, the simple apprehend but not
the wise of the world, for the reason that the simple attribute
all things to the divine, but the wise of the world,
attribute them to nature."
— Emanuel Swedenborg

I had the melody right away, but it took me well over two years to write this song: One, because it always takes me forever to write a song. Two, because I wrote numerous sets of lyrics until I settled on these simple lines and this, because I didn't altogether know where I was going. Three, because as in life, your path along the way is only made most clear when you've reached the end of your journey.

175

Chapter 41:
To Be Movin'

I hear my tires on the road
The wind is whistlin' my windows
Strapped to my seat... I don't care where the road goes
I've got no reason to hang around and so
I could end up in Mexico

Now I try and keep my spirits high
Though that's sometimes hard to do
I don't know why but it's true
I'm happy when I'm truckin' through
It's this constant battle... this same ol', same ol'
I think I'm losin' the fight
Still, it seems better to be movin'... just to be movin' along

From Maine to California... I've driven every road
Climbed most of the mountains
At least the ones that showed
I'll never get enough of this lovin' the road

Love's like the diamond and love's like the flower
Love's like the wind and the rain on the water
Love's like the freedom you feel in your heart
When you drive off the mountains and the prairie starts

Who'd of thought the Lord would have made it this way
With the mountains and towns and the scenery that plays
In my mind at night at the close of the day

It seems better to be movin'... just to be movin' along

I hear my tires on the road
The wind is whistlin' my windows
Strapped to my seat... I don't care where the road goes
I've got no reason to hang around and so
I could end up in Mexico.

Chapter 42:
Now That I'm Older

My life has no direction... I wonder what I do sometimes
The years just disappear... along with my dreams

My dreams assembled into song
That I could sing out loud when days were long
Incite some hope and light when hope was gone
As if someone could see the man inside

My life has no love... I don't trust the days anymore
My time for true love passed... now I'm all alone
As if someone could rescue me
From all the pain, the fears, the things I see
When people do their best to belittle me
She'd reach out with her hands and save all my days

There's a lot to admit to
How many lifetimes will it take and are left for me to see
There's a lot to admit to
Got to face the day... get off my knees

Now that I'm older
You think I'd give up these dreams... now that I'm older

My life has no direction... I wonder what I'll do sometimes
The years just disappear along with my dreams
I'm left alone... all alone.

I climb the canyon walls and from the ledges
Trace the river's ribbon to the sea
Like the wind that stirs...
There's a song inside of me.

Return to the Pinacate
Pinacate Preserve, Sonora Mexico

Chapter 43:
Return to the Pinacate

"I have it in me so much nearer home
to scare myself with my own desert places."

– Robert Frost / *Desert Places*

I return to Mexico, more out of a need to face my fear than a desire to walk the crusty lavascapes of the Pinacate. There is a spirit that is inherent to certain landscapes; this desert leaves mine unsettled.

My cowardice dwells in the tormenting nightmare of getting the truck trapped in the sands as I did the year before. The plan, this time out, is to do more walking than driving. I would stroll from here to the Gulf on a whim, but I don't want to motor one inch across this topography and become ensnared in the sand traps that clandestinely lie in wait. When you come to this depraved desert, you are out here all by yourself, complete, and completely alone. The prospect of getting stuck is real. It is with a great deal of trepidation I drive across this perilous expanse of rogue cinder and sand.

My first objective is to walk across the lavas to the "maar" volcanic crater Cerro Colorado, appropriately named in Spanish, Red Hill. The flaring cants of the corduroy, cauldron flag against the dusky desert to the southeast, as I move down the only road that meanders across the base and volcanic shield of the Pinacate.

I park the truck southwest of the carbuncle caldera by some miles and start my march. The promontory appears to be on the distant horizon in the clear desert air. Perhaps unattainable before the sun goes down, but a worthy goal.

Free as I cross the open desert. Well, open to the extent that I can see my destination but there are obstacles. When the volcanoes here were active, the magma moved across the broad valley creating a chaos of cooled-coulee barricades and labyrinthine terraces filled with fox holes and mini-canyons, near impossible to traverse and make any time doing it.

Fortunately, between bouts with abrasive rocky rifts, there are accessible cracked-pepper cinder-meadows where I walk unobstructed.

I cross a moonscape, barren and bleak. Gossamer strands of cirrus strain the sun's bright corona, a light breeze stirs wayward wands of ocotillo in the garish glare. Behind me rises the blue Pinacate. In front, the rutted rusty slopes of Cerro Colorado, as I peer into burnt-black pocket-craters where sunken gardens of spiky-silver cholla, prickly palo verde, whiskered senita cacti and the quirky stunted elephant tree, thrive in deep eight foot holes. Climbing in and out, up and over.

Astride the cleared pastures of crushed-clinker, I leave my mark on a fragile land. With every crunchy step, my boots break through the gruff exterior veneer, leaving a light brown dust, sole-shaped, contrasting the darkened ash. Conditions being as they are, these footprints will last a very long time and explains why ancient pathways, tracks and tracery, still remain.

With bullet speed, something lightning fast, disappears into a wall of palo verde – Sonoran pronghorn. They are quite rare these days and I'm surprised and pleased to see one – a fleeting glimpse, two seconds in duration.

The desert stretches sterile and stark and a red-chili hillock is rising. If I didn't know, I wouldn't know that it's the lip of a massive crater. The ruddy bluff concealing an excavation and a gigantic hole. The southern end of the heap is highest, a classic study in erosion. The bare-knuckled slopes deeply cut by desert rain over millennia. A lancing light, catching its faceted angles in sun and shadow.

An hour and a quarter, brings me to the crater's perimeter. Wonderful and odd, the outer boundary of the crater is completely devoid of plant life. Unlike the surrounding terrain filled with cacti and palo verde, nothing grows in a roomy ring around the russet slopes. It looks like it's been purposely cleared in an unnatural way, in this nothing but a natural place. I move across the peeled ground heading for the lowest section of the crater's lip.

With a gathering anticipation, up the gentle terra-cotta slopes,

I ready myself for the yawning space and the bottom to drop out of the top of this hill.

> *"We rode across the zone of ashes and straight up*
> *the side of a volcano. When we drew rein upon the rim,*
> *a gorgeous scene lay before us and the adjectives began to fly*
> *like hail. "Magnificent!" "Grand!" "Aesuvius in the desert!"*
>
> – William Hornaday / *Campfires on Desert and Lava*, 1907

On the swimming edge of a big blushed bowl, perhaps a half-mile across, maybe three-hundred feet deep the ground falls away. Unlike the other craters in the Pinacate, which are composed of over-cooked-coffee lavas, Cerro Colorado is unique, built of fine-grained red-brick ash. The ceramic compass, though heavily eroded, has a cheerier countenance compared to the other melancholic cavities that pock this desert.

Climbing down into the amphitheater, I walk to the center of the circus-ring and stare up at rubicund circling cinnamon walls and the one-eyed, wide-open sky, dense and deep, lupine-lavender-blue. I have strolled across a blank desert, dropped into a spectacular pig-iron vent in the earth's crust and I'm pleased with my shoestring accomplishment.
The sense of freedom and adventure is overwhelming. But nervous apprehensions and inquietudes chaperon inexpressive languishing landscapes to keep the heart fluttering between fear and exaltation. It is a preamble, to how I always feel here in the Pinacate.

This land of desiccation is a temptress, beckoning one to abandon good sense and just wander into its arrant idle quarters, but tempered with a perpetual ill at ease and accompanied with a loneliness that you carry about like a stone.

> *"A traveler sees many things which give rise to a multitude*
> *of feelings… some of them pleasing, some painful*
> *and yet others productive of wonder and surprise.*
>
> *This country is probably in the same state that it was ages ago*
> *Those who love the total absence of sound, and of the busy hum of*
> *man would here find a solitude so absolutely melancholy, that they*
> *would never willingly again quit the society of their fellow creatures."*
>
> – R.W.H. Hardy, 1826

Here at the bottom of the bowl lies a flat pan of creosote. Apart from a miniaturized palo verde here and there, little else grows. On the surface and in the deep grooves of eroded coralline rock, darker rocks and pebbles lay strewn about in different patterns, collections and populations, in the haphazard way that erosion works. But there is a master plan to this chaos, a symmetry and balance in this mineral-matter. I wonder at the way rocks of different size and weight come to rest where they do.

I climb out at a coffin corner and walk along the northern lip of the crater, which is as wide as a four-lane and just as hard. Metamorphosed: crouching sun shafts and shards, transform the abandoned stadium into a kindling-kiln all flare and flame. The surrounding desert views are grand as well. Stunning shades of majestic purple clad and cloak the mystic mounds of the Pinacate. Ambered sunlight floods across the flat, deadpan bone-yard expanse to the northeast, igniting every saguaro and a million perpendicular green sticks crowd the empty space. Distant sizzling, toothy Sierras reflect the closing light of day.

> *The complete unity of the desert under almost any light.*
> *The golden-crimson dawns, the fiery sunsets,*
> *seem to attune the desert and put all its elements*
> *into complete accord; but it also goes together*
> *as a piece from dawn to dusk with a different light*
> *and a different tone of color for every hour.*
> *The lilac, the rose, the golden envelope of air are in effect*
> *so many colored glasses through which we see the world.*
> *The mountains, mesas, and basins are all tinged by the prevailing*
> *hue or tint, and even the blue of the sky is tempered by it.*
> *The result is a color-unity in landscape the most astonishing ever*
> *seen. It is possibly this exact unity of tone that baffles*
> *the landscape-painter who would put the desert on canvas.*
> *Many have tried and very few have succeeded.*
>
> – John C. Van Dyke / *The Open Spaces*

I must hurry back to my truck before the sun leaves me to walk this desert in the dark. Down the cinnabarine slopes. (The question is; what color is this tilt and tip? It is ever-changing salmon-peach in tone, a pile of paprika, terra-cotta-cinnamon, a carroty-coral, bricky-flesh-tints-tawny-brown, burnished-bronze, hazelnut, henna, carmine-molten-metal and more and none of the above.) Across the wide treeless perimeter that rings the crater. Marching over the blackened-blue-maroon lava canyons to my truck.

> *"He was somewhere along the wild borderline between*
> *Sonora and Arizona, and the prospector who dared the heat*
> *and barrenness of that region*
> *risked other dangers sometimes as menacing."*
>
> – Zane Grey / *Desert Gold*

The sun is setting. I'm sitting on the bed of my truck boiling water for my freeze-dried dinner. Dawdling, long lapis lazuli shadows move across the desert now darkening-dim. A pickup approaches down the only road that leads in or out of this down-in-the-dumps desert and it makes me nervous. In my head, I run through the horror stories I've read and heard about the Pinacate. The ones about drug smugglers and guns and the people who don't come back; the threatening *banditos* who march out of the lavas with machine-guns, the ones who shoot first and don't care about the questions. People die out here. Obscene things happen.

Parked as I am by the side of the road; my only hope is, that we're all on the same side. The baby-blue junker has Sonoran tags and two Mexicans ride. They roll by slowly and stare. I wave a cheerful hello, filled with a false bravado. My body language, hopefully saying… yea, I'm cool… you're cool… I'm comfortable being here. I pray they keep going. They don't.

The truck stops and the driver opens his door… Oh boy, here we go.

"Do you speak Spanish?" he asks.
"No, I do not speak Spanish," I reply in a cordial manner.
"You don't speak Spanish!" he repeats condescendingly.
"What are you doing here? Where are you going?"

He's walking towards me. He's got a gun strapped to his hip… Wow, this really, really doesn't look good! What am I to make of this? What's up?

"I'll spend the night here. I'll cross the Pinacate tomorrow and sleep in Rocky Point on the Sea of Cortez tomorrow night," I say, hoping my increasing concern isn't showing.

"It is very dangerous here... It is not safe here... You should not stay," he says, in a kind of Cheech & Chong exaggerated Spanish accent.

I'm not quite sure if there's a joke coming, or he plans to pull his gun. He flashes some identification I can't read. He's with the Mexican Police. He doesn't look like one dressed in unkempt civilian clothes. But, what does one look like? No doubt, scouting-out the bad guys. He asks if I have a gun. They are not allowed in the Pinacate Preserve. "No," my reply. He talks of contraband, guns and evil men.

"It is so dangerous here... so very dangerous," he soberly says, with onerous south-of-the-border inflection.

What he is not saying: You stupid gringo... you have no idea how much danger you're in... No idea!

He looks over my backpack with a suspicious eye, peering over my side-rail at my stove and boiling water. He's laughing at me, though it doesn't actually show.

"So, you're telling me that I should leave right now?" I try and pin him down. He walks away getting back into the truck with his sidekick.

"It is so dangerous," he yowls, in his thick Spanish-English. "Go down to Rocky Point, but don't stay here... If you like your life – move on... It is so dangerous... so very dangerous," he keeps repeating. They drive off in a cloud of dust.

More has been "said," than has been said. The whole incident going down in just a few moments, very odd, discordant and patronizing... Now what?

Was this man a poorly clad Guardian Angel come to warn me of impending danger and doom, or is he busting my balls? Is something going down tonight that he knows about? Am I in the line of fire?

I know I'm in a particularly vulnerable position camped along this road. (If you can call this tattered track a road.) I worried over it before this sudden apparition. I sense the messenger is right. "He that hearkeneth unto counsel, is wise."

I pack up and drive forty-five miles through the dark to Sonoyta, cross the line and sleep in a safe American campground in Lukeville, Arizona. It is New Years Eve; fireworks celebrate my safe return.

It occurs to me that there are two deserts there in the Pinacate, a landscape over which two worlds collide. A huge empty tract of desert, that straddles two countries. A large monopoly board, where a serious game of under-the-table economics is played out. It's a smugglers paradise. The stakes are high and there are those willing to risk their lives and others as well, for that big elusive cash prize. The winners there win big and the losers lose everything. Money can be made and people are willing to try. Lives are lost in the push and pull. It has always been this way. It will remain so.

The Pinacate is also a place where desert-rats and dandies come to see its natural wonders, to walk the lavascapes and marvel. Who love it and hate it and fear it for what it is, barren and beautiful, sequestered and alone, appealing in its austere and aesthetic simplicity. The dolorous, sobering size of a waterless waste. A dangerous land, that dares the adventurer to come play chicken. The calculated risk one takes to cross it is half its appeal.

John Audubon Jr., son of the famous bird portraitist, traversed Arizona's southwestern deserts in 1850 en route to California gold. All though he lived to tell the tale, he never got over his fear of such forbidding landscape. His journey so profoundly effected his psyche, that even on his deathbed, the experience a decade behind him ranted about the desert he could not forget. The desert the one demon he could not put to rest.

There is a spirit that is inherent to certain landscapes. The Pinacate, like those deserts for Mr. Audubon, leaves mine unsettled.

"From the point of the believer, the purpose of emptiness and desolation is to prepare us for joy and ground us in hope. Unless joy and hope are the goal, the desert becomes a playground for masochists."

– Alan W. Jones / *Soul Making: The Desert way of Spirituality*

*"A great land
like a great lady,
has her way with men."*

– Mary Austin

Chapter 44:
The Walk

Leaves were turning October gold
The river ran slow with the summer grown old
Timbered shafts of sunlight... through slots of canyon fall
Where the water spoke of time... or was it nothing at all

Then the wind starts to blow... made the cottonwood sing
With the wind through their branches like a tuning fork's ring
And the raptors the same... come the lightning and rain
Then a still small voice... beneath the current of a storm

"Be still and know that I am God
I'm exalted among the nations... I'm exalted in the earth"
And with the tempests passing washed clean in bright light
Where the rainbow held sway
Proceed to navigate this river
Through a carved-stone hallway

But the way that wind blew... made the cottonwood sing
With the wind through their branches like a tuning fork's ring
And the raptors the same... come the lightning and rain
Then a still, small voice... beneath the current of a storm

And His words like music played
In the silent space between the thunders' parade
"I am the life... the truth... the way."

I've been wanderin' this desert just a little too long
Now, its time to climb higher
In the silence... epiphany... a vision... a song
Now, its time to climb higher
Time to climb higher.

Aravaipa Canyon

Chapter 45:
Aravaipa Canyon

In 1859, Henry Hutton, chief engineer responsible for constructing the "Leach Wagon Road" through the San Pedro River valley, wandered through Arivaipa Canyon and took a look around.

"This stream rises in the wide valley north
of the Playa de los Pimos, and
breaking through the San Calisto (Galiuro) mountains,
empties into the San Pedro. In the bends of the creek,
through the cañon, several small patches of rich bottom land,
which furnish a dense growth of large sized ash,
sycamore, iron and cottonwood timber.
Five miles above the gorge, the source of permanent water
is reached, being a large marsh, or lagoon, from which
a small stream, in many threadlike branches,
winds off toward the mountains,
The stream of "Aravaipa," was found to flow over a
gravelly and sometimes rocky bed, having the volume
of the San Pedro, with evidences through the cañon of its rising
twenty-five- or thirty-feet above its level, at the time of exploration."

Yesterday's storm has washed the air clean. Rain has polished the colors of the morning and strengthened the hues of all that the, now dazzling sun, ignites. The dreamy greens of the cottonwood, the intense blue sky. A sparkling stream-path leads me into the depths of an American treasure, Aravaipa Canyon.

Aravaipa (an Apache word that means "little running water") is a deep, wilderness gorge of banner beauty, about fifty miles as the crow flies, northeast of Tucson. Aravaipa Creek flows year round, a phenomenon in this desert land and water changes everything. A mini Grand Canyon built of multi-colored, multi-tiered, thousand-foot cliff walls that appear as wild as the day God made it. The canyon is about 12-14 miles in length and in the three days and two nights, one is allotted by the Bureau of Land Management, the goal is to walk the canyon up and back.

It's a hiker's heaven and a bird watcher's paradise with the ever-flowing water. Hawks, eagles and falcons fly the rock-rent-rhyming. A slue of desert song birds sing. Kingfishers machine-gun a warning ditty as you splash through your days. Sand snipes, egrets, and herons, angle the shimmering waters that support native fish populations. Mountain lions prowl, desert bighorn sheep ascend, coatimundi, deer, coyotes and javelina all make a comfortable living in this magnificent stone hallway.

On the southern exposed canyon walls, classic Sonoran Desert flora, saguaro cactus, rock and sun. In the flood plain, groves of cottonwood, willow, ash and sycamore, interspersed with green, grassy parks, cut in half by a ribbon of water. Along northern walls, where the sunbeams miss their mark, grand cedars grow in the cool shadows. The upper canyon walls are built of a creamed-coffee colored rock, sometimes sprayed a light green and yellow with lichen, where water pouring off the lips of unseen plateaus have stained the walls with black stripes, as though tar had oozed over its edges in a Utah looking landscape.

I have walked the length of Aravaipa four times, explored its major side canyons as well. Vergus is the only tributary gorge, yet unexplored. I'm determined to walk it.

Substantial alterations since I was there last. One of my gifts is an, all but photographic memory, when it comes to landscape. Having walked a given section of land, I will, almost without fault, cite the placement of every rock and tree. So it is with some surprise that I find the canyon's bottom completely rearranged.

Recent floods have pushed through the chasm with such force that it has scoured its flooring. It strong-armed the vast thickets of cottonwood and willow carving new watercourses, stacking up sandbars and reefs of river rock into small mountains. Great piles of flood debris cling to the trunks of grand old cottonwoods. Rat nests of twisted trees and broken limbs, showing the high watermark to be some fifteen-feet above the usual tranquil knee-deep flow of stream.

I had been thinking to myself, before I entered this canyon;

how does a submissive-stream of limpid-liquid like Aravaipa carve a clove of this magnitude? In witnessing the aftermath of this flood's strength, it's apparent; all it takes is time.

The day deliriously sunny and warm, an aspired meander. I haven't far to go. Five miles in, I reach Horse Camp Canyon and set up a bivouac. Here, where Horse Camp enters the main gorge, sits an attractively planted mesquite bosque set in the folds of canyon infrastructure, just a few feet above the rush of water. This park is furnished with ancient cottonwood and sycamore. A lush mantel of green grass carpets the ground filled with yellow and white spring flowers.

The place looks like the Canyon Lands of northern Arizona. Beige stone monoliths studded with cedar where saguaro cling to walls that rise eight-hundred feet. Cap-rock-corrals, crowding the river, creating a natural cathedral.

Vergus Canyon opens up at the opposite end of the park where I'm camped, about a quarter mile. That's on tomorrow's itinerary. For now, I head up the principle thoroughfare for a place called Hell Hole in search of desert bighorn sheep.

Without the weighty pack, my step is light. The familiar wave of euphoria sweeps over me as I drift down the canyon. This is my favorite section of Aravaipa: the compelling sculpture of the cracked and crinkled cliffs. The marvelous color scheme of the water-stained rims. Flowers bloom on high rock tiers creating a light dusting of gambogian snow. Increasing cloud cover forecasts a coming front. Winds rattle through the rock halls striking the age old groves of cottonwood that sing like tuning forks.

I spot a tribe of coatimundi. Deer graze at every park along the way. Ducks explode off the waters. Javelina hurry and hide. Hawks patrol canyon rims. On the stream shores, lion tracks cast in a maudlin mud mahogany-brown.

In the same location where I discovered desert bighorn on previous visits, I search the canyon walls once more. Sure enough, I determine seven sheep with none to shepherd. This time much higher up and farther away. You can't miss the bighorns and ivory rumps, as the small congregation hoofs it up on obdurate stone shelves. It's a thrill to see them; to know they're here and best to know where to look.

The first time I made their acquaintance, it was summer. Growing tired I planted myself in the sand to unwind. After a while, I realized that one of the rocks on the opposite side of the canyon, about twenty-five yards away and perhaps fifty-feet up on the first tier of ledges, had some very large horns; six sheep stood as statues. I was thrilled.

In the initial thirty minutes of observation, they never made a move, not a muscle. There were two females and three stately rams with trophy-size horns. A lamb played on a small jagged protrusion with its protective mother. The fledgling appeared vulnerable but already a steady climber. Though it seemed a lion could catch an easy meal in an unwary moment, ripened rams don't ripen, letting guard down.

I gloried in the moment. Watching them graze on mesquite, slipping in and out of sight behind rocks and brush. I could not believe my good fortune. Had I sat down twenty feet on either side of where I came to rest, I would have missed them completely.

I walk a few more miles up the canyon heading for Hell Hole, but it's getting late. I know a storm is coming. I'm prepared for it, but it's best to be warm and dry and in my tent when the rains come, as I must retrace my footsteps.

Reminiscing Hell Hole on the way back. All the side canyons there, are as individually unique and extraordinary as the main artery, with Hell Hole no exception. Layers of perpendicular porphyritic-rhyolite, hundreds of feet stacked tall and towering, with strange scallop-carved brims, as narrow walls plunge dolefully down into blue shadows. A clear, barely running, stream has melted its way through solid rock, singing its way through eternity. Stately sycamores, dwarfed by the chasm's confines, glow an eerie green, accenting the antic luminous immures, ignited by the slit of sky above my head.

Troops of coatimundi rained from the trees as I swung around the bends of stone. Bats bobbed in the sky windows above. Minnows drifted in clear water pools. The sound of the rocks and gravel, like broken china under my feet, echoed off the walls disturbing the silent sanctuary.

Caves poke-a-dotted the cliff walls. From carefully-cut grottos poured springs of living water, flowing from no apparent source, out of solid rock, that gave life to ferns and flowers and color-rich mats of moss.

I know a peace, the favored streams I walk. The Lord I hear when natures talking. His hand in all I see.

"Will anyone who thinks with any rational wisdom say such things (The created universe, and this copious canyon for example), arise from any source but a spiritual world, a world that the natural world serves by clothing what comes from it with a body, or presenting in effect that which is spiritual in origin?"

– Emanuel Swedenborg

Back at camp, I get a good fire going and enjoy dinner. At 8:30 P.M., the rain starts and I dive into my tent. It rains hard all night long. Warm and dry in my little cocoon, safe from the storm that rages just beyond fragile fabric walls.

With the morning, it is still raining hard. Nothing to do but sleep. Drift in and out of dreams for hours. There's a dent in the dowsing, around 11:30 A.M. So, having logged fifteen hours in the sack, I prepare breakfast through the open tent door and dodge incoming raindrops.

With breakfast concluded, I walk over and investigate the river. The, once quiet stream, is in a rage. What isn't a boiling seething rapid, is a smooth liquid conveyer belt and moves with the determined weight of an unstoppable runaway train. That a night of rain could produce this great a transformation, is a revelation. Just the water pouring out of Horse Camp and entering Aravaipa is unnerving.

Walking down to Canyon Vergus, for I had hoped to trek it – a complete wash out. Water-jets jostle through house-size boulders. Great trees stand mid stream, trying to hold their own against percussive, calamitous currents. I can barely hear myself think above the whitecap-water-weave crash and careen. Again it starts to rain. I head back to camp.

The afternoon is on and off again showers. Nowhere to go,

I dare not leave the safety of the park's high ground. To cross the river would be complete foolishness. It would sweep my life away as a leaf upon the wind. I'll have to sit tight.

Nothing beats a good storm. The alluring landscape in which I find myself is enhanced by the glory of the tempest. Cascades spout and spill, tumbling off the dizzying heights of every canyon rim. Splashing and sliding down the rock faces, adding a splendid coloring to the masterfully-chiseled walls. The canyon resonates with the sound of great waters as a hundred cataracts plunge to the river. It's like the first day of creation, the wild wet gardens of the canyon, like an Eden planted. To experience Aravaipa now and this weather, is to understand how this sanctuary was fashioned, for it was born of water.

In the wilderness, there is nothing but time. I spend it walking. Trapped by the water's tantrum, nowhere to go, I realize how much time there really is. Between periodic bouts of rain and hail, I stand by the river and watch the muddy waters rise.

At 4:00 P.M., another deluge begins and for two hours a gushing torrential hurricane rain. I debate building an ark. If this keeps up, I'm going to need one. Nothing to do but sleep. Rising at 6:00 P.M. with a good omen. For fifteen minutes before the canyon grows dark, the underbelly of the cloud ceilings spark with the fire of the setting sun. The storm is losing its grip on the canyon.

Far too wet for a fire, in the darkness through the open door of my tent, butane flames boil-up a bowl of oatmeal. Ringtail cats frolic about my camp. One races right up to me within inches. They are as bold as they are beautiful.

Morning births a new day and cloaks it with a blue sky. I get up late and stake the river that I might gauge the waters as they recede.

Fortunately, the cataclysms in Vergus appear in retreat by a smidgen. I forge the flows and battle up the canyon.

Vergus walls look like those of the main canyon. But its flooring is filled with mansion-sized boulders thrown down from the rim rock. It's a damn tough go, one obstacle after another. Where I can, I bid the waters and climb the boulders. Where I can't, I push up the canyon sides pressing through impossible mesquite thickets. Forced to retreat after a distance, short of having ropes to climb the two-storied boulders, I can't get around the surging waters or the jungles of growth.

Vergus is stunning. Water keeling over the tawny rims above my head. White veils of water gush through every boulder barricade. The charging waters over the centuries have carved and polished deep, stone gutters. Torrents dash down the rock sluices in a joyous romp of swirl and sway. I lunch in the warm sun, beside a whizzing water-slide and watch hawks float on upwelling currents of air.

Back at camp, my stake on the river indicates no change in water level. The floodwaters move with a strength and resolve that deflates any daring I thought was mine. But growing tired of this park, I brave a river crossing, for there is more room to walk and explore on the far shore.

I search for the safest intersect, deciding on the widest section with the least rapids. The swift waters are above my waist and it takes all I have to hold my own against the careless current. The river bottom has a life of its own, a treadmill of moving sand, rock and gravel that attempts to pull the rug out from under me. It's a high-wire balancing act to the far side.

Climbing up Horse Camp Canyon I get the visual thrill of this excursion. Unlike Vergus, this ravine is boulder free. It's a massive stone sliding board that slips off a series of terraces. Water fills the whole of the canyon bottom and skips off big stone steps roaring like Niagara; an outstanding water show.

The potent power of the plunging water creating a great wind that moves down the canyon, carrying with it a billowing mist sifted from the surging sea. Rainbows strike their colors against the clouds that race by sun showering me till I'm soaked with river rain. Where water isn't tumbling, it rushes across pretentious, polished-rock tables heading for a fall. All plant life, be it humble grass or proud tree, bowing to the boasts and brags of wind and water.

Climbing out of Horse Camp, I walk for several miles up the main drag. With a watchful eye, I study canyon terraces, hoping to spot something move. Late afternoon sun finds mule deer sitting like statues on high grassy slopes. They hold still, thinking I don't see. The stealthy lion plays a better game of hide and seek. I settle for fresh paw prints pressed and molded in the mud at my feet.

I stay on the outlying shores of the river as long as I can, but cross I must. After another long search for a safe breach, I enter again the river caldron. This time I barely make it, being pushed far down stream to reach the opposite strand.

My stake on the river indicates that the waters have actually risen through the course of the day. At dusk, I stand at the confluence of Vergus and Aravaipa and worry over a demented jumble of brown rapids. The ferocious whisk is moving with such force, that it's pushing bowling ball-sized rocks along the river bottom. I can hear them striking against each other as they're swept along with the tide. There is no way I could enter this earthen-deliquesce strapped to a backpack and survive. I may well be trapped there for a few more days.

> *"… I recall John Muir most distinctly, a tall man with the*
> *habit of talking much, the habit of soliloquizing.*
> *He told stories of his life in the world, and of angels; angels that*
> *saved him; that lifted and carried him; that showed him where to put*
> *his feet; he believed them. I told him one of mine:*
> *except that I didn't see mine. I had been lifted and carried;*
> *I had been carried out of the way of danger; and he believed me."*
>
> – Mary Austin

I stoke a cozy fire and eat my last dinner. A three-quarter moon lights the canyon as though it were day. Beneath the shadows of cottonwood canopies, I stroll through the blue night. Silver moonbeams gild canyon walls that gleam like polished chrome. Despite the problems with the river, it's hard to be put out of countenance filibustered by such beauty.

Snug in the folds of my down bag, I listen to the roar of restless waters. Far above my head, I can hear the somersaulting cataracts in Horse Camp Canyon echoing off the rock balconies that sound like jet planes thundering; the whole canyon ajar with the quarreling voice of water.

The good Lord willing, the flood-tide-tumble will turn. I'll brave the river tomorrow and hopefully live to tell of it.

And so it is. The river has dropped a foot by morning. For breakfast, I eat my last morsels of food; a cup of hot cocoa, five slices of salami, two slices of Swiss cheese; sustenance to assess my situation and weigh my options.

One thing is certain. Having watched the weather forecast before I came, another big storm would follow the one I've just endured. Should it come before I make an escape, I could be this canyon's prisoner for a long time, without food.

Unbeknownst to myself, at this very hour the Pinal County Sheriff's Department the Nature Conservancy Ranger for Aravaipa and Arizona Search & Rescue are meeting outside the canyon debating whether to send in a chopper for my rescue. After some deliberation, they decide to wait until 5:00 P.M. to fly a helicopter many a mile in from Tucson. It's a dangerous job plucking the thoroughly shipwrecked from deep cut canyons, floating on the precarious winds of whirling blades. If it can be avoided, they'll do so. They decide to wait. I'm determined to conquer the river.

It's another glory day in Arizona, the sun bright and warming. A marvelous mat of lush green grass cloaks the park about my tent and is saturated with a million delicate white and yellow flowers. Hawks, on the hunt, drift above the canyon skyline. The river's verdant woodlands scent and musk the air with cottonwood and willow. Colored canyon cliffs tower.

Break camp, and stash my pack under a tree. To kill some time, I cross the river where I did the day before and climb back in to Horse Camp to check out its tumbling Niagara. The volume still formidable, but its flow has been reduced and that's good news. Back across the river for my pack and I'm on my way.

For a staff, I have a well-chosen piece of driftwood. I'll use it as a third leg to keep me balanced against the rowdy-water-war and as counterweight to my cumbersome backpack, also as a probing tool to search the bubbling-bottom for holes. Cautiously, I enter the river. I make it across – just!

I walk the shores as long as I can and cross the river when necessary. Each time, using all my strength, I'm just holding my own against the swift silty spate. Tremendous relief, having successfully crossed. Equal portions of fear and trepidation when I must, once again, enter the dark swilling water. I come to see myself and the run-away-river as equally matched wrestling contestants. All it can throw at me and all I can muster to resist, bringing me step by step down the canyon and closer to home.

Two sections of the canyon frighten me most. Places where the walls completely close in on the river. With nothing to hold onto, the waters roll silent and deep, funneling down long corridors of stone. Having entered the perilous passage, there's no escape but the other end. If something goes wrong there, it would be a disaster. Strapped to a backpack, it's hard to tread water and fight this raucous and ruinous-drift.

Well, it's a push and a shove this turbulent tide, but enter the hallway I do. Whirlpools, spinning and ebbing, appear and disappear, driven by ominous manipulating undercurrents beneath the surface. The waist-deep waters grow progressively deeper. About halfway through I can no longer sound the bottom with my staff. The unstoppable water propelling me along. At the point of no return, I take a broadening breath and close my eyes, fully expecting to plunge to the bottom like a diving bell. As if by a miracle, my feet find the only high ground in this flooded flume. Never sinking beyond my upper chest, I make it through, while all around me I cannot fathom the river's bottom with my staff.

I toil down the canyon, a few more turns, a few more bouts, with the river. Coming around a bend, I poke my head above a large boulder to find a woman standing at the water's edge.

As I swing around the rocks, traveling not twenty-feet, I'm spotted. Racing up to me as an uninhibited, inquisitive child, she peppers me with unending in-culpable questions – incessant. "Are you walking out of the canyon? Have you been crossing the river? How far have you come? Have you been fording these wild-waters? Would you take us with you? Please wait! Please take us with you! Please take us with you!"

Another girl appears. Together we walk over to their camp and exchange our stories and experiences of the last few days;

the storm and the rising flood waters.

It is quickly decided that I will help them escape the canyon's crimp, guiding them to safety through tempestuous river torrents. I am a knight in soggy shining armor come to a maiden's distress, an answer to earnest prayer. An angel sent from Heaven, commissioned of God as to their safekeeping. I'm pleased to be of service. Judging by the near panic in their eyes, I'm just what the doctor ordered.

The girls have had a rough go of it. They have been trapped in the canyon for five days. Two days before, they had fallen in the river with their packs. All that they carried got soaked. With waterlogged sleeping bags and tents, with wet clothes, they struggled to keep warm and dry against the night's cold temperatures. Caught by the stream, frightened by a river, soaked to the skin; it has not been fun.

Karen is thirty-nine years old and a seasoned backpacker. Average good looking, perhaps five-seven, with light brown close-cut curly hair. I have an instant rapport with her. Karen has walked in the Sierras of California, as well as the Canyon-lands in Arizona. She's walked many times in Aravaipa and is knowledgeable in horticulture and archeology; we have much in common.

Penryn is twenty-five years old and a green horn, an eastern tenderfoot. Before this outing, she had never spent a day in the wilderness. She has not had a good time. I find Penryn attractive, comely and cute, her dark hair frames delicate girlish features. Penryn's whole manner reveals a guileless childlike vulnerability, I find appealing.

The thing about wilderness backpacking, apart from the obvious beauty, is that the whole process of the walk from the beginning to end is a vision-quest. Tremendous physical demands are placed upon you. You are forced to make decisions. The right ones complete a successful journey. A wrong one could bring disaster. The emotional highs and lows can be extreme. In the end, a kind of revelation, but only in the end. During the whole process it's damn hard work and it often isn't fun; time and again you just want to turn back, give up and go home. Only after the chastening, suffering and affliction you discover of what you are physically capable and so completely renewed and refreshed in spirit, that for a week after the trial and tribulation, you are convinced that nothing is impossible in your life. But you've got to get to the end.

Penryn has not been able to get with the program. She's been an emotional wreck for days. With the storm and waters rising, she's had a running battle with tears, bouts of depression, hopelessness and fear. At junctures so despondent and desperate, as to do something foolish like enter the river before its time or leap from a cliff wall to end it all. This girl is on the edge.

Karen on the other hand, has been wise enough to know that there is nothing to do but wait for the waters to recede. She's done her best to keep Penryn calm for five days. It has not been easy. They have spelled a big "HELP" with rocks on their sandy beach, hoping a delivering helicopter might descend. Short of that, they planned to wait one more day before braving the river. Karen has shown herself the wiser.

Now with my propitious arrival, there is great relief. A light has appeared at the end of a tunnel. Perhaps this ordeal will soon be over. Frantically they break camp, stuffing all they have as quickly as they can into their backpacks. All of us talking at once and worrying over what obstacles lay ahead.

I give the girls a crash course in river walking. How to brace themselves against the crushing current and how to plant their feet for sure footing on a river bottom that stays in continuous motion.

It's no wonder the girls were so intimidated by this part of complicated river snarl. I try, unsuccessfully, in several spots to cross. What isn't over my head, is a rapid so swift and strong I can't stand against it.

One option is to climb on a ledge a few feet above the surge, clinging to a shear rock wall that crowds the deep water pools. Now balancing myself on this shelf for a few feet and dropping in on waters I hope won't be over my head, this being rather difficult with an unwieldy pack. Before I drop over the ledge and disappear from the girl's view, I tell them to sit tight. "If its safe and I can cross the river, I'll be back for you.

Just sit tight! I'll be back!" I vanish behind the rocks.

I lower myself into waters that are a foot above my belt. Struggling to the far shore I take off my haversack and head back for the girls. As I sight across the water Penryn is on the ledge and ready to drop in on the river. The look on Penryn's face is one of absolute terror. Paralyzed by fear, she cries out in this defenseless, panic-stricken voice, the pure desperate sound of which I will not soon forget. "Don't leaves us Drew!... Please don't leave us!" This girl is on the edge.

I race to her side, assuring her that won't happen. She drops into the drink and clinging like a cocklebur we move across the water as one. Planting Penryn firmly on the counter-coast; now requital for Karen, and we two make the crossing.

Foiling the river there proves a precedent, the heroic hurdle. Sometimes just getting started is the hardest part. Were on our way down the canyon, walking on the shores where we can and crossing the river when we must.

Penryn is so excited with the prospect of getting out of this five-day ordeal she can't get out of the canyon fast enough. When on firm ground, she is practically running down the beach to the next crossing. Then, waiting pensively by the chastening whirl of wild water where we all cross together. This girl is on the edge.

Karen, on the other hand, hurt her leg with the first crossing, not badly, but she's bringing up the rear. I'm in between, trying to keep the two ends of this line tied.

We ford the fearsome flows together. I lead the way, probing the boil and bluster with my staff. They, holding on to each other, hold on to me. Sometimes we get halfway across and are forced to retreat, in search of waters, more circumspect. Calmly, methodically, we make our precarious journey down the canyon.

The ladies have put me in a wonderful position. They cannot stop thanking me for having come to their rescue. All that I would like to be; they believe I am. They have picked up on my steady, rock-calm demeanor. They constantly flatter. Telling me how brave I am. They can't believe how unruffled I appear under such stressful conditions, that as a savior I have come for them. Confiding complete faith and trust, with a total abandon, as only a child can. Adoringly, they hang on my every word. A mega boost for the ego. They have given me a power I have rarely experienced so consummately; thrilled to be of service.

The last crucible, test and trial, the place I feared the most. The second great hallway of shear rock walls forming an inescapable corridor. So intimidating was the look of the water as it funneled down the deep long wend, insidious, reckless and raging, it gave us all a start and startle. Marching along in single file like elephants, each holding the tail of the one before, the storm-surge shot us like bullets through a rifle barrel. Landing at the end of the lengthy passageway unscathed, the worst of the river behind us.

With a few more turns of canyon and complement river-criss-crossing, we reach an embouchure where colossal clefts open wide. We have made it. Here, walls retreat to broaden the valley. The river now, less restricted seems less threatening. Two-and-a-half miles to our cars and home.

In the mists of one of our river skitters, we look up from the wrangling waters to see three people approaching. These strangers seem mighty glad to see us! We say hello and make our introductions.

Ted Grooms is a rancher who lives at the mouth of Aravaipa. Working closely with the Nature Conservancy, he has been in on our planned rescue. A helicopter has been flown in from Tucson. At 5:00 P.M., just twenty minutes from now, it will fly up the canyon to save us from the floodwaters. Ted started up the canyon to see if we might be coming. Now, having found us, he suggests we hurry along and try and catch the whirly-bird before it takes off.

Mr. Grooms is as nice a guy as you would ever hope to meet, an engaging handsome blond, with a winning bright smile. Electric-blue eyes peer out from under the rim of a fabulous green Australian safari hat, with a black-and-white checkered flannel shirt that compliments his now wet khaki trousers. Luscious leather boots, the kind for which I would give my eye teeth. He is without doubt, Arizona's best-dressed rancher, looking like he just stepped out of the pages of an L.L. Bean catalog.

Everyone is talking at once. They, because we have been found, are asking us more questions than we can answer about our ordeal. And we, having been sequestered in this canyon for what seems a near eternity, inquiring of news from the outside world.

Ted brought along two ranch guests, Mark and his eighteen-year-old son, Kevin. All want to know what wildlife we have seen and how we managed to escape unscathed, the turbulent waters.

Ted explains that in the years he has been living there he has never seen the Galiuro Mountains so packed with snow. That the storm we weathered deposited a thick wintry blanket of the white on the plateaus beyond these towering cliffs that now confine us. The authorities were convinced that the eighty-degree days would melt the snows so quickly, the river-ought-rise even higher, making a difficult situation worse.

Awash in a brilliant blast of late afternoon sun, we make our last river crossing. Ascending a mini-bluff, afresh a large, fenced field, tabled above the troubled waters heading for the ranch house. Flowering cottonwood forests have sent a billion floater seeds to drift in the refined and perfected air, a blizzard of tiny round feathers beneath sincere blue desert skies.

Six of us string out across the wide paddock. I dawdle and dally with Penryn, the caboose in the caravan. She confides in me; how frightening this experience has been for her. How, out of hope, she had reached the depths of despair. How desperate her prayers, how lost she felt when help didn't come. How, as an angel of mercy, I had appeared in their mists.

At the halt of green pastures, we climb a steep hill on the top of which sits dapper Ted's ranch house. As we labor up the sharp rise a reeling red helicopter whizzes over our heads moving about the canyon on its aerial mission to save. Waving our arms, we signal the pilot that all is OK. Making a big loop, he tips his hat and heads fifty miles back to Tucson.

The haughty hacienda has a commanding view of Aravaipa Canyon. It's a surprise to see the Galiuros layered in deep snow and it moving all the way down to the terraces above the river. While the cottonwoods of the river bottom are August green. It was quite a storm. A majestic landscape made all the more appealing with the addition of snow.

We pile into Ted's Land Rover for the short ride to our waiting cars. In the parking lot, we meet the Nature Conservancy Ranger for Aravaipa Canyon and a Sheriff from Pinal County. They ask us the obvious questions. They make sure that we're all right. Though I can tell that they are a little peeved that we have put them to so much trouble. We apologize, and thank them for their angst and considerations. All is well that ends without a drowning.

In closing, the ranger related his adventure of the day before. Alarmed the river was on the rise and worried for our safety, he battled up the canyon in hopes of finding the disinherited. In the long stone corridor that filled us with dread, in waters shoulder-deep, he was forced to retreat. He knew then we were in trouble and was frightened for us. He began planning a rescue.

Karen wants to treat me to dinner. It's decided we'll stop at a Mexican eatery in the small town of Mammoth as we venture home to Tucson. The drive out of the canyon is spectacular. The rugged Galiuro Mountains, snow-filled. The desert floor, a patchwork-quilt of striking blue-purple lupines that rug the hillsides with color. Lavender air hangs over remote white Alps that trail into the distance.

From a booth in La Casita, we peer through the picture windows across the San Pedro River to the frost-frozen Galiuros. We discuss our timely escape from Aravaipa. It's been a real adventure. Compliments continue. "Oh, Drew, you're so brave... so strong... so steady." I would like to believe them. One is rarely placed in a situation where help is so desperately needed. I've gotten more out of this than they, humbled and honored to be of service.

With dinner relished we say goodbye. The euphoric drive back to Tucson. Through the dark and the flicker of headlights, I can see tumbling cataracts as they pour off canyon rims the morning after the salvo's cannonade. Desert bighorn sheep dancing on high rock ledges, the roaring Niagara in Horse Camp Canyon. Those scary, determined floodwaters, the absolute terror in Penryn's eyes when she would confront the river, the fearless ringtail cats that wandered my darkened campsite, fresh lion tracks pressed into gooey brown mud and more. Deer silently watching from the sylvan greens of skirting parks hemming the "little running water."

Aravaipa is magnificent. I wouldn't have missed the storm for anything. The fact that I have conquered its Noah-like deluge and inundation and lived to tell the tale, has made it all the more rewarding; a vision-quest complete.

It's a call on Canaan land…where a Jordan flows
Through tabernacled canyons… basilicas like Rome
Searching pilgrims come … for the New Jerusalem
And to scan the view… now look how far I've come.

Aravaipa Canyon

Chapter 46:
A Long Way to Go Before I'm Home

Tall blue mountains stand… these prairies they roll green
Braided silver threads a river runs
A distant city shines… beyond the distant sun
With a long, long way to go, before I'm home

Sailors man their ships… on great waters ply their trade
A captain steers by faith for stars
Alone to chart this wilderness… I chase the dream I made
With a long, long way to go, before I'm home

Let the storm roll in… let the river waters rise
Fill those high mountain meadows with snow
Angels I believe… they've been whispering in my ears
Keeping fears and dangers at bay
"Be strong and be of good courage… neither be dismayed"
Now set thee on thy way

Tall blue mountains stand… these prairies they roll green
Braided silver threads a river runs
A distant city shines… beyond the distant sun
With a long, long way to go, before I'm home

Just a long, long way to go, before I'm home.

Chapter 47:
The Walk Out

*"Honor the work of man; honor to those who spin
and carve and build; honor to the hand that rounded Peter's dome;
but what of the hand that rounded the earth and established
the blue dome of the sky, what of the work of the great builder!"*

— John C. Van Dyke / *Nature for its Own Sake*

Something happens to the spirit when it tests itself against mountains and revelation at its culmination.

Deeper than canyons, older than mountains, I would that I had wings.

I would that I had wings and appear like an angel at the top of a ridge. Walking blue corrugations, over forested mountains, into the depths of lonesome canyons, to light by streams, beneath whispering fir canopies, finding a rest and a joy in the work of His hands and a peace beyond this beauty, deeper than canyons, older than mountains.

I would that I had wings.

I write this at the end of an ark of walking. From the Chisos Mountains along the Big Bend in Texas, to the lavascapes of the Pinacate in Mexico, from the basilicas of Zion in Utah, to the endless forests of the Leopold Wilderness in New Mexico, across the Mogollon Rim, to the red rock cathedrals in Sedona. From the Kaibab Plateau, across a Grand Canyon to the peaks near Flagstaff and south to Patagonia, from the Kofa Mountains in the west to the Chiricahuas in the east, I've left few stones unturned.

I have shared here, but a few of my walks and a few of my songs. Concentrating on my own backyard. And in reviewing my journals, I see – less is more. Another story, becomes one more magnificent indistinguishable canyon. A dreamscape is like that. Exceptional Arizona is less a locality and delineation on a map than a compendium and geography of the spirit.

For the Southwest is at least as much a place in my head and heart as it is a place in reality. The reality is so rewarding and it is the foundation on which I have set a large portion of my life.

All I ever wanted to do was to write songs and take a walk somewhere. The world is not interested in such craziness. Walking Arizona has provided me an unending adventure and a wellspring of song writing inspiration. It is a station steeped in an eternal beauty, an undying mystery. It is theater for the imagination. I have let my feet and my mind wander.

I am the least practical person I ever met, as evidenced from the fact that I am on my fourth decade of writing songs, with the full knowledge that no amount of talent, determination or dogged pursuit of my goal can bring this dream to fruition as working reality. I remain undaunted for one reason only. It is a natural calling; I wouldn't know who I was if I couldn't pick up a guitar. I have pursued my craft with an honest and pure heart for the shear love and joy of doing it.

I have pursued walking with the same enthusiasm, for the same reasons. It is a natural calling; I wouldn't know who I was if I couldn't take a walk. For me, there has always been an inherent emotional and spiritual response to landscape which pulls me into it like gravity. I am enamored with the art-filled allure of landforms; it is nothing short of religious experience. Any interesting landscape would do. Preferably a western landscape. But if I lived in Scotland or Spain in Appalachia or Argentina or call the tune, my life would be the same. I would be walking and fashioning songs. The walking and the writing go hand in hand like a marriage.

The adventure of walking lends itself to romanticism. The glory of creation lends itself to spiritual inspiration. The act of walking fetches a clear mind. My natural joyous response to all this beauty is spontaneous melody.

Fortunately, the artist has license to create out of things around him that which he will. Living in Arizona has given me a lot to work with, a large and diverse canvass from which to draw. But the wonderful wistful-world I have created in my own imagination is at least as real as the real, wonderful world and sometimes, it's hard for me to distinguish between the two.

Sadly, there are things I dislike about the Grand Canyon State as well, mostly man's doing, things I wish I could change, but my impractical artistic outlook allows me to overlook the unpleasant and see only the beautiful. The futility of writing songs, now and then, comes and slaps me up-side the head and this disquieting realization, proves to me how much I am living in a province of my own fabrication and how much there is I cannot reconcile.

Arizona remains an extraordinary location for an extraordinary number of reasons, and for all those reasons, I love it with spunk and pluck, as directing principle and polestar. Its history, ancient and new, its people, the blend of cultures, architecture, religion, God's handiwork on a grand and diversified scale, the amorous smell of it when it rains. I was born for the place. I am certain, if you took out of the equation my love for singing and writing songs, this wayward-walking and Arizona itself, my life would cease to exist, at least as I have known it or ever wanted it to be.

The physical and emotional high that comes with the march and the miles, is an intoxication born of the enchanting beauty that encompasses and what happens to the spirit over time, as you participate with intricate landscapes like these. There is revelation in walking and under these conditions any man can find himself. It's that still small voice I've been listening for. It's led me out this door and down these roads. And having reached this physical plateau, although genuinely tired, there seems no limit to my ability to walk endlessly onward.

However, after three decades plus of the habitual hinterland plod, I fear there may be somatic limits as to how far one can walk, or even needs to. With the strength of my better years behind me, I carry battle scars as a result of the hard won miles, arthritic knees and a deteriorating will. Though I pray the Good Lord will give me the brawn to continue, for I literally would not know who I was if I couldn't take a walk. And my life and music never make more sense than when returning from a good jaunt. But I've done my job, climbing every canyon ridge and peak and loved every aching moment.

I can close my eyes and drift up a hundred dazzling unimaginable canyons, over every mountaintop, across deep valleys, impassable rives, to a resting-place, unto hallowed-hills hushed and hiding.

A delve of legerdemain, magic and memory. Bright reverent mornings, brilliant afternoons spent in sunlit glory. The resplendent sky embers of evening, never the same, ever the same. Clear nights filled with campfires and a billion distant suns. Traipsing abandoned dry, dusty deserts. Strolling enchanted mountain forests. Forging diamond-rivers. Sauntering prairies rolling perfect. Listening for psalms in tabernacled canyons.

I know of secret springs in the mountain passes, where clandestine waters tumble through a canyon's crinkle. Where large fish drift like dirigibles in deep water pools. Where carved, color-rich stilettos of stone stare down on belittled groves of cottonwood, never visited. Where covert timbers, have been aging for a thousand years in the clefts of confidential canyons. It seems I know every nook and cranny. I can float in and out of these locations at will and often do.

I see art. I see great beauty. I see the divine in natural things. I know a peace, the favored streams I walk. The Lord I hear when natures talking. His hand in all I see. My being *Swedenborgian* in my outlook explains quite a bit.

My purpose in writing, was simply an excuse to talk about beautiful things, the art of this creation and a passing note on the spiritual implications of landscape. And this thought, that has so enhanced my appreciation of nature and has lifted my mind above the merely natural things placed before me, which in and of themselves are marvelous and remarkable beyond words.

In short, there is an inherent spiritual correspondence with the natural formation, which is a match and immaterial-metaphor, an allegory reflecting a deeper spiritual reality.

Apart from the singularly striking and uncommon components that make this a magical land. I love Arizona first and foremost, for the art of the place, the shear esthetics of this creation. For I dream of western skies, the color of the air and the light in the canyons – that bend in the river where the cottonwood grows – that's where my memory flows and my heart won't leave. I am less an artist than I am one who appreciates good art and sees it in most everything. From the exultant to the mundane, everything in my eye has an aesthetic purposeful balance. And like all good art, everything is wrapped in metaphor and the more I look the more I mark and mind.

The very act of walking is its own metaphor and is analogous to a walk of life, with profound spiritual implications; a potent parable when walking across a desert to a point of water.

For Arizona is just a pile of rocks, though it be- a beautiful pile of rocks. And if beauty, all that could be found here, that would be enough on which to be content. But there is more to this than meets the eye. The things placed before us, are representative of deeper spiritual realities not always made manifest.

If, "Nature is the art of God," to quote Thomas Browne, then landscape is saturated with spiritual simile. For what artist worth his salt, could be satisfied with painting just the natural objects he sees, insisting these things portray and delineate the esoteric. Nature is the glove a spiritual hand is wearing – the natural world a foundry for the spirit.

If passed masters use parable and metaphor to discern and disclose, then surely the Supreme Artist, the source from which all things spring – and in whom we live and move and have our being – has fashioned nature in such a way, apart from the obvious purposeful practicalities of creation and if understood in its proper light, as a kind of spiritual metaphor to reveal a higher truth. If we could lift this material veil, we would then comprehend clearly, that in every created thing hatched and brought into existence, there is something reflecting our Creator, His divine intentions and ourselves expressly. For God is a perfect man and we in His image. Everything fashioned reflects this truth. "Therefore, all nature, is a theater representative of the Lord's Kingdom."

Sometimes, until a statement is made on a given subject, it doesn't become a tangible idea on which the mind can rest.

Just as music is pure emotion put to melody and the emotional response to it, moves us to the crux and core of our being. As great art lifts the spirit and the mind of man in higher import, a pith-noble-essence and weight, beatitudes beyond oneself, so the art of this creation is doing the same. And this spiritual tugging at our hearts and this emotional response to beautiful things, as when we stand by a river, or walk through a forest, or look up at the mountain, is both a conscious and unconscious, reciprocal interplay, between the Creator and the created.

"If mountains reflect celestial love and the hills below them, the spiritual; if natural water, corresponds to spiritual truth; if rocks, signify faith; if animals, reflect (man's) varying affections and the trees, perception and knowledge; birds, intellectual things; if gardens, groves and parks, intelligence." Then landscape becomes a stage integrating a metaphysical parallel reflecting a measure of meaning in purpose and plan, an analogue, like an image of God in a mirror, a place where natural mountains and rivers are spirit condensed.

This grand sweep and wide array of diversified landscapes that Arizona has to offer, makes this school of thought all the more dramatically pronounced and poignant.

Is it possible to walk across a desert land and upon discovering a seep or a spring or a flowing river and not be impressed by the resonant spiritual implications of such a phenomenon? Not in the trappings themselves, which are wonderful and remarkable, but in what ethereal substance they represent. This celestial component is the ingredient that satisfies and a truth that wends me on my way.

And so, I remain captivated, by the intricate tapestry that is Arizona. I am drawn by the shear weight of its brimful beauty and this tangible, spiritual correspondence, to walk *This Gloryland*. The aesthetically pleasing and comprehensive sweep of this creation; its worthless creosote deserts, the symmetry of its forested mountain skylines, its graceful prairies, its shining rivers, the proportionate arrangement of these contrasting parts. The pleasing impressions of its size, colors, and forms, have come to rest on my mind like a melody… With a melody in mind.

Intensely and affectionately moved by this splendid art

coming into being, I can't help but, within me see, cunning spiritual occurrence and circumstance the more I gaze, contentedly, this natural painting. This pleases my spirit to no end and makes me think and ponder beautiful things.

Something happens to the spirit when it tests itself against mountains and revelation at its culmination.

Deeper than canyons, older than mountains, I would that I had wings.

I would that I had wings and appear like an angel at the top of a ridge. Walking blue corrugations, over forested mountains, into the depths of lonesome canyons, to light by streams, beneath whispering fir canopies, finding a rest and a joy in the work of His hands and a peace beyond this beauty, deeper than canyons, older than mountains.

I would that I had wings.

Who'd have thought the Lord would have made it this way,
with the mountains and towns and the scenery that
plays in my mind at night at the close of the day.

Cabeza Prieta

You'll Find the Road as Long

Chapter 48:
You'll Find the Road as Long

Hope dims… like the miles so far behind ya'
You'll find the road as long

The dreams you chase… that still can't seem to find ya'
You'll find the road as long
When twilight's doubting haunting hunts and hounds ya'
You'll find the road as long
The promise and the pledge coin the fears that undermine ya'
You'll find the road as long

And like the dreams you know
They're God-givin' and ya' go
A walk entrust… a still small voice to follow
When earnest prayers ring tinny-tin and hollow
Trip the lie… you'll never-ever go the distance
A gamble and a dare and christened solitaire
You'll find the road as long

A call to faith… not a friend you'll find beside ya'
Come near to courage on a course that now confines ya'
When earnest prayers ring tinny-tin and hollow
When you know you'll wait as least until tomorrow
You'll find the road… you'll find the road as long.

Bedouins and nomads –
they know my freedom
These dreams like earnest prayers
unanswered yet.

Stone Altars

"I only went out for a walk,
and finally concluded to stay out till sundown,
for going out, I found, was really going in."

– John Muir

Chapter 49:
Snow on the Santa Catalinas

It snowed on the Santa Catalinas today
Bright sun on the clouds as they faded away
Left the snow line high above the desert floor

In the spring… there's a flower on everything
Arizona has this smell… you grab yer girl and yer dream
At night….. a soft, warm breeze up from old Mexico

I'll hate to leave this place… I'll hate to leave this town
I'll hate to go back home and stop this wanderin' around
I've got to go back east… I've got some work to do
In coastal canyons, I'll be workin'… I'll be dreamin' of you

You… where the clouds that Rincon-mornin'
Crashin' into the mountains as the thundershowers came
And I… didn't catch or heed the warnin'
Started lookin' for shelter
But got caught out in the rain
When I finely found some rocks to house me
I hid there… till the rainbow came

Now you can keep the city… there's nothin' for me there
Give me a stretch of open desert… and I don't much care
Still can't say what I want… but hope to find it there

It snowed on the Santa Catalinas today.

···

Every time I hear a whistle blow…there's a tuggin'… tuggin'
Stand by a river, it's then I know… there's a tuggin'… tuggin'
The Catalinas in snow… a desert blooming below
Every time I walk a field that's sowed
There's a tuggin' at my heart
Every time I hear a whistle blow.

"As they age, all things grow rigid and bright,
The streets fall nameless and the knots untie.
Now, with this landscape, I fix; I shine."

– Robert Desnos

Chapter 50:
Blessed Beyond Measure

Every day it's the same old thing
I climb into these canyons
And I sing… sing… sing

I'm blessed beyond measure… with family and friend
And a dream each day to work on
There are mountains to climb… and the fun never ends
I'm blessed beyond measure my friend
Blessed beyond measure

I'm blessed with the morning… the black night, all stars
And a new dawn to start my day in
For this glorious sun on my sill come to play
I'm blessed beyond measure that way

I'm blessed beyond measure… to follow that which I love
For the joy in the fields I'm working
But unto summits – abiding a sojourner tends
I'm blessed beyond measure my friend
Blessed beyond measure

I'm blessed with the calling… the promised glory that waits
And the storms through the sylvan valley
For the carols I hear and the songs that I play
I'm blessed beyond measure that way

Don't break the spell of my inspiration
Don't take away the dream
An epiphany waiting in the mountains
Revealed in the river and the sunlight beam

Make every day the same old thing
I'll climb into these canyons… and I'll sing… sing… sing.

My dreams assembled into song
That I could sing out loud when days were long
Incite some hope and light when hope was gone
As if someone could see the man inside.

223

"Tell all the truth but tell it slant
The truth must dazzle gradually,
Or every man be blind."

– Emily Dickinson

*"Like all great travelers, I have seen more than I remember,
and remember more than I have seen."*

– Benjamin Disraeli

"I dream my paintings,
then I paint my dreams."

– Vincent Van Gogh

Credit Where Credit is Due

This book and many of my songs could not have been written over the years without the continued insight and inspiration derived from author John C. Van Dyke (1856-1935), who wrote with such artful eloquence about *"The Desert."* He showed me how wonderful words might be cobbled together in praise of beautiful things. An art critic who explained in a tangible way what I knew instinctively, and yet did not completely recognize, until of course, he wrote it down, what it was that my aching heart so loved about *This Gloryland.* His observant eye and admirable prose cannot go unmentioned here, for he, in the end, is the real artist in this book.

I have also, been profoundly moved by the Swedish philosopher and theologian, Emanuel Swedenborg (1688-1772). I have alluded to his theory of "Spiritual Correspondence," in this book. The quotes in *"Beautiful Things,"* and *"The Walk Out,"* are his.

Ralph Waldo Emerson described Swedenborg: *"A colossal soul who lies vast abroad on his times, uncomprehended by them. One of the mastodons of literature, he is not to be measured by whole colleges of ordinary scholars."*

Henry James, Sr. wrote: *"The incomparable depth and splendor of Swedenborg's genius are shown in this that he alone of men has dared to bring creation within the bounds of consciousness. He grasped with clear and intellectual vision the seminal principles of things."*

Helen Keller called him a *"Titan Genius, an eye among the blind, an ear among the deaf."*

I have thrilled to his theology and believe it worthy of investigation, both by the believer and non-believer, the scientist and the intellectual, or a simple man of faith such as myself.

Just as John C. Van Dyke taught me to see that the landscape itself, is a painting. Emanuel Swedenborg taught me to see that the artist, exquisitely manipulating the natural canvas, finesses all with a spiritual hand and in measures divine.

I have thrown in a few obvious Bible verses for good measure.

227

All songs were written by me, with the exception of *"Far Trails,"* – the lyrics I share with cowboy poet and author, Henry Herbert Knibbs (1874-1945). Quite by accident, I stumbled onto his words when I was working on this song, *"Far Trails Await Me,"* which fit perfectly into the melodic change I had already written. An immaculate match that finished the song and the rest, as they say, is unrecognized history.

"Hill Tops High and Fair" is an anonymous poem I discovered in *"Streams in the Desert,"* a compilation of inspirational writings by Mrs. Charles E. Cowman, published by the Oriental Missionary Society in 1946. It spoke to me immediately, not just because of its sentiments, but because it expressed it in a way that I would not have imagined expressing. Even good poetry rarely makes a good song. I added a few lines of my own to make it one; it remains one of my favorites.

In the year 1205, Wang Wen-wie wrote: *"The Fashioner of Things has no original intentions."* Of course, this is ludicrous on its face, for who builds a house without original intent? (Without the why and what-for, why?) But, he also wrote something profound: *"Mountains and rivers are spirit condensed."* And who could argue? For the Lord hath not made the spiritual world and all things in it, out of nothing, but out of Himself (The Divine of the Lord, is love and wisdom, life itself, substance, shape and form itself, uncreated.) and the created natural world and all things in it, through a kind of, spiritual condensation.

If I could spell, I would consider myself an educated man. Sadly, this is not the case. I thank Daisy Willeford, long time resident of San Manuel and the San Pedro River Valley, not only for her wonderful stories about the Galiuro Mountains, but also for her assistance with this manuscript and in helping me get things right.

Anybody who thinks they can write needs a good editor. I found three.

Thanks to Evaline Auerbach, for her adept assistance as I wandered about in my unsettled search for appropriate words and making essays: *"A River Sometimes Runs Through It," "Blue on Blue," "Snow in the High Country"* and *"The Fire Fight,"* worth the fight.

A huge thanks to godsend Constance Taylor, for taking the impure carbon of my manuscript, pressing, squeezing, cutting and polishing; that it should glitter and shine diamond-like.

Kate Horton – a consummate artist, illustrator, editor, book-designer and all around whiz-kid on the computer – she has made *Gloryland Reprise* the piece of art I dreamed it could be.

"Man & Wildlife in Arizona," – The American Exploration Period, 1824-1865, by Goode P. Davis Jr. is a wonderful history book, recording what some of the early explorers found when crossing Arizona for the first time. An excellent source for wonderful quotes.

I thank the Good Lord for just about everything else, for the freedom and strength to walk *This Gloryland*. For the loving and supportive fortunate family I was born into. For warm friends found, who have shared the dreams of songs and the glory of mountains.

Stacey Jo Cohen, translated *"Ocotillo,"* as,
"She finally Spoke Spanish to Me."

Way up north, they've got that snow
and the cold wind blows
Think I'll take a trip
and winter down by Mexico
I'll climb into some mountains,
drink from canyon streams – lost somewhere.

Drew Signor

Drew Signor is also the author of
"Sweat of the Sun, Tears of the Moon"–
Thirty years of Songs, Essays and Insights,
the Artist and his Craft.

He has devoted more than forty years to
songwriting and performing, over thirty years exploring
Arizona backcountry, singing songs of the wilderness
and the spiritual implications of landscape,
of truck drivers, Appalachia, and
the love that's waiting at home.

He currently resides in Benson, Arizona.

Gloryland Reprise . . .
offers incomparable peace and beauty,
an insightful look into the art
of our creation and its spiritual presence
through song, prose, poetry, and
cunning illustration as he investigates
southern Arizona's hinterland.

Drew Signor

Kate Horton

Kate Horton is the
graphic designer and illustrator of
"Gloryland Reprise."

When asked by Drew to get more involved into his book
besides just formating text and chapters, I saw a chance to
renew my old habit of pen and ink drawing
like 'back in the day' when a camera was not the
tool like it is today to record your space on this planet.
His love of the Arizona desert and its critters
fell right into my way of thinking
as well as the spiritual feelings of nature.

She currently resides in Oracle, Arizona.

Gloryland Reprise . . .
offers the artist's impressions of the
plants, animals, mountains, rivers,
and deserts of southern Arizona.
It is another way to pay homage to
nature and use art to bring these
quick sketches to others.

Travel the world on the back of a worm,
Seeing all you can see,
Learning all you can learn
And pray that the moon doesn't melt away.

A List of Drew Signor Songs

Some songs in this collection can be purchased at https://www.cdbaby.com

You can also listen to some of Drew's songs at www.youtube.com/Drew Signor

Gloryland Reprise

Walking the Southern Arizona Wilderness
and the Spiritual Implications of Landscape

"This is the place our parents never warned us about.
The hot ground where if you enter, you can never leave.
Drew Signor shows us the way to leave the house
and find our place. The heat, rock and white light
that burns this place into our minds
and flesh bring forth many songs.
Listen up, as one lover explores
the heartbreak hotel of our dreams."
– Author Charles Bowden

"In his book of essays, "Gloryland Reprise," author and
songwriter Drew Signor offers an appreciation of Southern
Arizona's wild regions as rich and evocative of "place"
as Joseph Wood Krutch's "The Desert Year"
or Aldo Leopold's "A Sand County Almanac."
– Casa Grande Dispatch

"A compilation of essays and song lyrics written by
transplanted Pennsylvanian who now lives in Benson, where
he is captivated by the desert. Signor is a veteran hiker
who's not averse to driving a truck when he can. His accounts of his
travels contain as many travails as spiritual epiphanies –
he is an honest diarist and a conscientious researcher.
His chapter "Sierra del Pinacate" is worth the price of the book.
– Arizona Daily Star